Warriors of the Forest

The Beaver Wars

Ford C. Balch

1/1/2011

Factitious characters have been developed to dramatize historical events in this story. These characters will take you through the period known as the "Beaver Wars" (one of the main characters, Ahatsistari, is based on an actual Huron Indian). Events are listed chronologically to help demonstrate an escalating warfare. Victory is influenced by weapons supplied to Indians, and their demise is seen following contagious diseases they suffered. The saga ends with the displacement of Indian tribes and the loss of beaver supplies. This book, also, depicts events of the Indians gradual, yet continual loss of land, and traditional life and practices to an advanced European culture

Acknowledgements

I dedicate this book to my wife Lena, whose understanding and patience allowed me to work on the book, alone in my office.

I would like to thank Mrs. Yvonne Gadway, who constructively read the book and suggested one inclusion which I had shunted off so I went back to the story and followed her suggestion.

I lack words of appreciation to express sufficient gratitude to Mrs. Jean DiSabito who edited the story and spent many hours making it into its final version.

I received the inspiration for writing about the Mohawks from the Six Nation Indian Museum in Onchiota run by the Faddens, and where the true history and culture of the Iroquois is preserved.

Ford C. Balch

Warriors of the Forest

The Beaver Wars

Copyright

1st edition January 2011

Self published

By

Ford C. Balch

Indian pass used by the Indians

to go through the Adirondack Mountains

The Mohawk Trail - Western Massachusetts

Indians in wait

Indians Fighting

Table of Contents

Warriors of the Forest - The Beaver Wars

Indian Brave

The Munsee (Delaware) tribe
The Oneida tribe
The Onondaga tribe
The Poosputuck/Unkechaug tribe
The Seneca tribe

The Cayuga tribe
The Erie tribe
The Laurentian tribes
The Mohawk tribe
The Mohican tribe (including Wappingers)
The Mohegan tribe (including Montauk and Shinnecock)

MAP – New York State Indians (ca. 1620)

Indian War Dance

Warriors of the Forest - The Beaver Wars

Prologue

In the first volume of a two volume series, life of the Iroquois Indian in the year 1600 AD, prior to the introduction of European culture, is explored. When the Europeans arrived, they found a Woodland society who obtained their food, shelter, clothing, weapons, and tools from the forest. Their weapons were far inferior to the Europeans, who had passed from the Copper Age into the Iron Age.

In the second volume, devastation that the Europeans wrought in the inevitable clash between the two cultures will be examined. Disease ravaged through the Indian tribes. The introduction of firearms, and the need to obtain new beaver ponds to maintain the supply of furs for the Europeans, caused increased tribal wars, many times with French or Dutch as their allies. The Beaver War, also known as the French and Iroquois Wars, took place in the mid-17th century, when the French, Dutch, and English supplied rifles to the Indian tribes who served the Whiteman's interest.

Sitting Owl returns in 1613 in the second volume, now 25 years of age, and through his frustration, you will witness the changes that will effect, and intrude upon their woodland life.

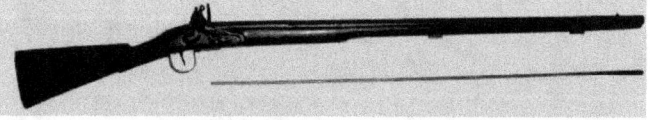

Chapter I - Eagle Dance (August – 1614)

Otstungo (Mohawk Village)

Sitting Owl entered the ceremonial lodge for an Eagle Societies Dance.   He wore an eagle feather, which had been given to him years ago by the dew eagle,iii1iii, (a supernatural creature that flies above the earth.) While Sitting Owl watched in a dream-like state, the dew eagle filled the sky with his size as he came close. Then taking Sitting Owl aloft, he showed him leading and healing his people. After Sitting Owl received this vision, he was invited to join the eagle society who was responsible for the health of his people. The eagle was their symbol since he flew high over the earth. He looked down at all creation below, and would notice anything wilted or sick and in need of care.

Sitting Owl carrying a wand (specially prepared stick with four horizontal eagle feathers, each attached parallel), and a rattle sat beside some of the braves already there. In front of them was a forked pole with a stick hanging from it, that would be used to strike the ground. The rest of the group filed in after Sitting Owl. The Leader put a water drum and rattle beside him, then appointed needed assistants: a Caller, a Priest, Speakers, and a Presenter of Wands to the Dancers. The ceremony began when the Leader offered a prayer of thanks to the Great Spirit, and then with the Priest, sanctified the wands and rattles by throwing tobacco over a fire. A wand is given to the Priest and Speaker.

The Caller signals for the dance to begin by calling out. The Leader strikes the drum twice, and the first song begins. He is joined by another person shaking a rattle. Fourteen songs will be sung, each started by the Caller, and continued until the stick is removed from the forked pole, and struck on the ground ending it. The Leader will also strike the drum signaling the song's end.

---

[1]

14

The Speakers address the crowd with testimonies of cures, prayers for health, and thanksgiving.

There is no dancing for the first three songs. On the fourth, the dancers sway on their seats waving wands with arms stretched, and shaking rattles imitating a bird on a perch. When the drum increases in beat, the dancers will jump to the floor and dance crouched turning side to side, moving wands and rattles in time with the beat. For the second time, drums quicken, and dancers intent on grasping the corn with their mouths, lunge toward the food in the center of the room, shoulders weaving back and forth, wands and rattles held far out to the side. Dancers return to their seats with the food, now imitating a bird feeding upon its corn by twisting their bodies and looking around.

The dances are short, but song and dances are repeated until someone strikes the pole on the ground. The dance is repeated for each of the remaining ten songs. The end is with the Leader collecting the wands and giving thanks to the Great Spirit and Spirit Powers.

Dancing was strenuous, and Sitting Owl was thankful for the breaks when the ground was struck with a pole. At the end of the dance, a feast was available for everyone. (Laubin, 1977)

The Eagle Dance

By George Catlin (1796 – 1870)

id of manners, customs, and conditions of the North Americans

Chapter II - The Feast

Running Doe, with their new born child strapped in a papoose, joined her husband Sitting Owl. "You danced very well", she said as she sat down.

"Thank you", replied Sitting Owl looking at her admiringly, thinking how lucky he was to have her for his wife.

"I wish you were not leaving in the morning to take furs for trade at Fort Nassau", she said.

"I am going with Bent Feather, who also has furs, and we both wish to obtain a knife that will allow us to skin the beaver more quickly. I will hurry back, and will bring a kettle back", replied Sitting Owl.

Sitting Owl knew he could make much better time going by himself, and that he would be back with Running Doe and their newborn within a few days. When spring came, he would take her with him, and let her look over the glass beads and rolls of cloth found in the trading station.

Bent Feather joined them while the table was being prepared for the feast. He was fourteen years old, and the youngest brother of Running Doe. Bent Feather and Sitting Owl hunted and trapped together. Ears of corn were set on the table with hominy cakes moistened with juice, cornmeal bread, apples, wild cranberries, berries, and nuts. Squash had been baked, and venison and bear meat were supplemented with rabbit and squirrels killed by the older boys in the camp.

After eating, Sitting Owl left with his wife and child to return to their lodge. Bent Feather said he would follow soon, but wished to talk with some of the youths who had returned from a war party in the north.

"Do not stay up too late as we must leave early in the morning", said Sitting Owl.

Upon entering the longhouse, Sitting Owl put two logs on the fire. He was tired from all of the strenuous dancing, and fell asleep in a few minutes. Running Doe sat by the fire, and for a time, stitched deerskin into moccasins. She wished that she could make an excuse to keep Sitting Owl home, for she had an ill feeling---one of foreboding. She was preparing for bed when Bent Feather returned and went to his bunk.

Chapter III - Fort Nassau

Running Doe went with Sitting Owl to the river the next morning, and together they watched the sunrise. A red haze appeared over the horizon, growing in intensity until the clouds overhead became red and yellow. This was followed by a white ball which rose in the sky, and quickly chased away the darkness.

"It will be a gorgeous fall day", said Running Doe. Forgotten were concerns that she felt the night before.

From here they could look at 'the Noses' where the river twisted and turned in convolution seeking escape through the high limestone cliffs on both sides. Riding the updrafts created by winds and looking like a tiny spec was an eagle. The eagle would perch on the cliffs where it's nest was located. Here, the Indians would camouflage themselves using roots woven together, and they would wait for an eagle to land. Then they would grasp the eagle and pull out the tail feathers. Many times Sitting Owl would climb the cliffs and watch the eagle soar high above, circling and untouchable in its path of vigilance.

Furs were placed in the center of the dugout canoe, Bent Feather sat in the front. Sitting Owl got in the back and pushed the canoe from the bank with a paddle. Running Doe sat on the bank, and watched them until they disappeared from view.

Taking advantage of canoeing the river down current, they stayed close to shore and observed wild life along the river banks. A mink slid into the water and came up with a fish in his mouth. A blue heron stood in the water, paying little attention to the canoe. Tag alders grew along the river banks and made passage to the river difficult. It was in the shade, that Sitting Owl could see flashes of silver in the water receding under the river banks.

By noon they approached Schenectady village, and they both knew it would not be far to an island where the trading post was located. After landing the canoe at rivers edge, they were met by villagers who insisted they eat with them. While being served their meal, the villagers visited with them. When they left, the two knew that they would not be able to reach the trading post by dark. It was dusk when they reached the spot where the Mohawk joined the Hudson River. Here, at a 70 foot water fall, they found an empty travelers cabin. They gathered fresh balsam bows, and laid them on ground to sleep upon.

This water fall was called the Cohoes Falls and it was believed to be the site where Degana-widah survived a fall from a tree into the torrents, and presented the Good Message to the Mohawks.

Cohoe Falls

They reached the Trading Post the next morning.

The Trading House: The first recorded European Structure in New York State, built in 1614, known to the Dutch as Fort Nassau

© L. F. Tantillo

Sitting Owl was amazed at the site of a clipper ship moored off shore. It had three large masts that towered high in the air with sails waiting to be unfurled, and ropes straining against their moor as if seeking the freedom of the open sea. Inside a palisade arose a building that was 26 feet wide by 36 feet long. The stockade outside walls was 58 feet square, and it was surrounded by an 18 foot wide moat.

Bent Feather and Sitting Owl dragged the canoe far enough on the island to be secure, and then started to walk toward the board ramp that crossed over the moat. They were met by a stocky white man who had a welcoming smile upon his face. He raised his hand as a symbol of friendship.

Both Indians raised their hands as they appraised the white man. He wore a wide brim hat, a top coat with a wide collar, and a sashay tied at the waist. He wore shoes with stockings to the knees and knickers from the knees up. A sword was secured in his sashay.

21

Dutch Traditional dress Public Domain

Sitting Owl pointed to the furs indicating that they came to trade. The Dutchman made a sign back of acceptance. The Indians followed him through the palisades on a path leading to the trading post. On the grounds was a tall pole with a flag waving gently in the breeze. It was divided into three horizontal bars-red, white and blue. Three men and an officer stood in line, facing the flag. It was time to change the guard, and these three would be marched by the officer to relieve the three that had been on guard duty since 2AM. Sitting Owl was quick to notice the military preciseness and watched the men obey the calls of their officer.

Their guide patiently waited until the men marched off and then with a smile said, "come" motioning them toward the door. Sitting Owl looked in amazement at the inside of the building. On the walls and counters were an assortment of supplies: ax heads, knives, awls, bolts of cloth, glass beads, woolen blankets, kettles, muskets, ammunition and powder. He ran his finger down a knife blade, and took two off the counter motioning for the trader to take his pelts. Most of the items were exchanged on a per pelt basis[iv] (a beaver pelt would sometimes be called a beaver blanket). He also took two ax heads. For Running Doe, he picked kettles, awls, beads and some cloth. Bent Feather, who did not have a wife, picked up a musket. It was a smoothbore matchlock. The trader showed him how to light the wick so when the trigger was pulled, it would bring the wick down to the powder in the flash pan, and ignite the charge in the musket's barrel.

Sitting Owl joined them and said to Bent Feather, "It looks like your target would get tired of waiting for you to get ready to shoot it".

Bent Feather replied, "Should we meet a bear on the way back, stay in back of me, so I can make an accurate shot". Having decided to get the musket, he also obtained a supply of powder, musket balls, and a horn to hold the powder.

The Dutchman followed the two to the gate, then turned to Sitting Owl, and motioned to himself, and said "Wilhem DeGroot".

Sitting Owl, pointing to himself, said "Sitting Owl".

DeGroot looked at the Indian, noting his upright posture and direct gaze. It was free of the deceit and treachery that comes from greed for worldly possessions.

When Sitting Owl reached Schenectady, the villagers saw him and his friend Bent Feather, and called for them to stop and eat. It was only mid-afternoon, so they decided to keep going. Soon they came to the village Teatonaloga, on the Schoharie Creek named after a village called Schoharie, that was located further up the creek. Again the villagers offered them food and lodging to stay overnight. When they entered the camp, they saw a pet bear that was being fed scraps of food by the Indians.

"Ha", said Sitting Owl, "There is a bear to test your musket"!

Bent Feather looked at his friend but decided to say nothing. They told their new friends what they had seen at the trading post. Bent Feather added, "The trader will take all the beaver pelts we can get".

Sitting Owl said, "Our father's ways were good ways. It is easy to use a deer hide to cover up ourselves, and get close enough to use our bow and arrow. One musket shot will scare the deer close by, and they will learn how to avoid us".

23

He watched Bent Feather, but could see that Bent Feather was not about to give up the musket. The Indians fell silent because the table was now loaded with food.

After the meal, the chief of the village, Dark Cloud, addressed the group. He told how the younger Indians were trapping as many beaver as they could find. "Orenda, the Great Spirit, is sorrowful when he sees how we abuse what he had put here for us".

The villagers agreed it would become more difficult to find all the beaver pelts the Dutch wanted.

"Yes", said Sitting Owl, "We may have to go into the foothills of the Adirondacks to find more trapping places to continue to supply the white man with more pelts".

At sunrise they were up, and on the path toward the river to return to their village. As they went through a clearing, surrounded by trees, a bird glided a few feet over their heads and disappeared on the other side.

"Did you see that?" asked Sitting Owl.

"I did", replied Bent Feather." It looked like an owl flying from a tree".

"Sitting Owl said, "I fear this is a bad omen. It can only mean trouble ahead. Let us take our knives and axes, you take your musket, and put them where they will be readily available".

The villagers wanted the two to wait until a party could be gathered to accompany them to the next village, but Sitting Owl was too anxious to return to Running Doe to wait. He and Bent Feather set off on the river. It was still light when they approached 'the nose'. Bent Feather motioned to land the canoe.

Once on shore, he said, "Let us climb the ledge and take the trail to the village. It is quicker than through the twists and turns of the river". The two hid the canoe with brush, and Sitting Owl left a kettle and cloth underneath the canoe until he could return for it.

After reaching the top of the ledge, they rested while eating a piece of hominy cake. Bent Feather grimaced as Sitting Owl gave him one of the alder* fruits to chew, assuring him that after he ate it, his muscles would no longer feel tired. *<not recommended by author>

They stopped at the launching site, where a few mornings ago they had begun their journey down the river and through the 'nose'. Sitting Owl knelt to the ground, exclaiming : "Many braves have landed here since our departure". The two rushed toward the village, no longer trying to hide their movements. "Here", said Sitting Owl, "they came from the river up the gulley and came out along side of the village".

"Un-huh", replied Bent Feather, sharp eyes missing nothing! They entered the palisades and viewed the damage.

"Ah", exclaimed Fighting Buck, one of the older braves. "The Huron came and got inside without anyone seeing them. They killed many and carried many away. Everyone fought, even the young boys and old men. Red Feather is expected back with his war party and will chase the Hurons".

Sitting Owl tensed, but Fighting Buck restrained him with his arm. "Running Doe is gone. She was down at the river in hopes of seeing you, and there was no sign of her or the baby after the Hurons left".

Bent Feather said, "We must wait for morning, and then the two of us can track them. There is nothing we can do tonight". Sitting Owl grudgingly agreed.

.

THE FUNERAL

Chapter VI - The Funeral & the Chase (August 1614)

Sitting Owl could not sleep. How he wished his grandfather, Grey Wolf, were here. His grandfather had been War Chief for a long time, and his greatness in battle was remembered at the council fires. Finally he fell asleep until in the early morning hours, he was awakened by Bent Feather,dressed and ready for the trail.

Bent Feather spoke, "I believe that some of the main party went out by the gully, crossed the river and headed for the St. Lawrence over land, and that this group should be followed. Let me leave first and I will mark their trail when I find it, and it will be easier for you to catch up".

It was still dark and Sitting Owl was asleep again before his friend had left the house. He awoke with sunlight, and the sounds of voices outside. Collecting the glass beads, he went outside to join others on an a hill adjacent to the village.

Fighting Buck greeted him, "I did not expect you, Sitting Owl, but am glad to see you".

Sitting Owl replied, "Bent Feather is already looking for their trail, and when he finds it, he will wait for me to join him later".

Fighting Buck said,. "Since he was a boy, he has had no equal for tracking. The Huron will regret having him follow them".

The Indians dug a pit four feet deep. Bark lined the floor and the fallen were placed in a kneeling position with hands before their face, and knees drawn up. Faces were turned towards the west. Sitting Owl dropped his glass beads into the pit. Others left arrow points, turtle shell rattles, and clay pottery. After all the offerings were placed inside, bark was placed over the bodies, then the dirt was replaced.

Sunset was near as Sitting Owl began to prepare for the journey that he would start in the morning. He filled his quiver with arrows and took one of the new knives and axes. He packed enough food to last a few days on the trail, and lying down, he fell asleep until he was awakened by a blue jay's raucous cry of protest as a squirrel collected seeds from the ground. Streaks of light began to brighten the horizon.

Bent Feather found the Huron's trail. It went west up the valley, until it turned to go up a stream, one of many flowing into the Mohawk River, and part of a drainage system from a huge watershed. Bent Feather was familiar with this river that started far back in the mountains from a small Adirondack Lake. It twisted back and forth in a wild and rugged wilderness with rapids where the river dropped through mountain canyons.

Bent Feather came to a clearing, and set up camp. He would follow the Huron, but would try not to get too close until Sitting Owl had joined him.

The Hurons had also stopped at this spot the previous day.

"Hoy", said Little Stone. "You worry too much Lame Duck. The Mohawks have war parties away fighting the Algonquins in the Northeast Adirondacks. We will leave the Mohawk River and follow this stream that flows into it, called the West Canada Creek.

We will divide into two groups. The first group will go up the creek until we find a place suitable for ambush. We will wait on the ridges until we are sure no war party has been organized. Meantime, the others will go into Fulmer Creek, located farther up the Mohawk River, and hide a short way up the creek, so that they could fall in back of a war party, in case they should appear".

"It sounds good", said Laughing Gull. "We will wait until we are sure that no one is following, before leaving the creek to rejoin you. So should the Mohawks give chase, we will be close behind them".

A young Indian came forward and addressed the group. Although he was only 14 years of age, he had already proven himself to be worthy of the war trail, and was known by the others as Ahatsistari[v]. He said, "I would be glad to stay in the back and watch for any Mohawks that might follow".

This drew quick approval, and Little Stone started up the West Canada River. Ahatsistari left with Laughing Gull to go to Fulmers[vi] Creek and hide in a dry creek bed that was protected by its clay bank, and surrounded by a mingling of blue and yellow asters and goldenrod tassels in their fall colors.

Ahatsistari and Laughing Gull were watching when Bent Feather started upstream, leaving a signal to show the way.

"He must expect someone to follow", said Laughing Gull. "Take two or three braves and follow behind him."

Ahatsistari left with two companions and was close behind when Bent Feather stopped to prepare his camp for the night. Bent Feathers had hoped that Sitting Owl would have caught up to him by now, but figured he must have been delayed at the village. Although Sitting Owl was not as familiar with the Southern Section of the Adirondacks into which they would be entering, he was very adept for survival utilizing his surroundings.

Bent Feathers thoughts returned to his sister, Running Doe, and he was unaware that three pairs of eyes were watching from the woods as he drifted off into sleep.

The sky was beginning to lighten with a red glow, when three shadowy figures slipped into the clearing. Bent Feather stirred and felt a spearhead prick against his side. "Rise slowly as I do not wish to kill you", spoke a voice. Bent Feather looked at the Huron braves standing over him, one holding a spear in his hand, and another holding his musket.

The one with the musket asked Bent Feather, "Why do you follow us by yourself? Who is in back of you that you must mark a path to follow?"

Bent Feather replied, "I mark the way to lead a large war party that is most likely underway by now".

Ahatsistari scowled and retorted, "Your sign has been removed. If they follow us up this creek, the fox will become the hare, and be eaten."

Bent Feather remained quiet; for it seemed he was about to be taken captive, and there was little he could do about it.

Sitting Owl approached the clearing later that day. He skirted the field before entering, and found Bent Feather's bed-site. He could see that Bent Feather left with someone, and with a sinking feeling, he realized that he must have been captured. If they took a captive, they must be ready to return to their home. To follow further by himself would be futile; upstream the woods became cut up with ridges, gullies and windfalls. With a heavy heart, he turned to go back to the village for more help, and would return later to take up the trail.

When Sitting Owl returned to Otstungo, a war party, with Red Feather, had returned from the Susquehanna, and were angry they had not arrived earlier to fight off the Huron. They had joined the others grieving for the ones fallen and missing.

"What can you tell us Sitting Owl?" they asked.

"Bent Feather is now their prisoner, and maybe Running Doe is as well. I have come for help, and want to follow them as far as necessary."

"We will join you Sitting Owl, and it will not take long for us to be ready."

That afternoon the braves painted their bodies and began the war dance. Bending and twisting, their speed increased as they danced until they were tired; then they stopped to rest and eat.

That evening Sitting Owl slept fitfully under a star-lit sky. The stars grew dim as clouds began gathering, and grew into thunder clouds with flashes of lightening. A vision appeared and drew closer. A stallion with wings reared in front of him, then he heard a voice commanding him to "get upon the stallion's back". He grasped the mane and it flew among the stars above the clouds. The clouds would break so that he could see the ground, and then seal together causing darkness. Finally the clouds disappeared, and Sitting Owl could see the ground and feel the presence of another in back of him. The stallion landed and Sitting Owl got off.

A voice said, "Do not despair, Sitting Owl, perilous times are ahead and you will see many battles. Your people will depend on your strength to guide them through the many turmoils ahead. Do not forsake the Great Spirit in your future travels".

That morning at sunrise, Sitting Owl spoke to the braves assembled in front of him. He briefly mentioned his dream and said that their journey might be lengthy with battles, but in the end that they would be victorious. Then he crossed the river, and wasted no time in getting to the clearing where Bent Feather had been taken captive. Three days had lapsed since his capture. Sitting Owl was concerned that the trail was starting to grow cold.

Sitting Owl studied the trail left by the Hurons, and asked the rest of the braves. "Does anyone see anything suspicious?"

"Yes." spoke Red Feather along with several of the others, "It is too well marked and looks like a decoy".

"I agree", said Sitting Owl, "They do not think that Bent Feather would follow by himself. They expect us, and we will watch the backdoor and be on guard."

"AHa", said Laughing Gull, as he watched the Mohawks leave the clearing, and head upstream, "The hunt will soon begin. Unknown by them, the hares will soon be chasing the fox, Let us wait for a little bit, then follow until it is time to drive them into the others."

Sitting Owl surveyed the valley where the river and the trail curved together, coming close to a ridge along their side. "If I were their leader, I would pick this spot for ambush, because the valley is narrow." He led the braves, leaving a plain trail until halfway near the bend, then they turned and veered to the side to hide in brush, taking care to cover their trail. Laughing Gull , deceived by the well marked trail of the Mohawks, hurried to drive them into the waiting Huron. When the trail ended, Laughing Gull stopped, he was confused.

Ahatsistari kneeled by a tree with the musket he had taken from Bent Feather. When the Mohawks sprang from hiding to attack them, he fired his musket at the first brave who came into view. Sitting Owl felt a lead musket ball buzz by his head, and heard a low groan; then a body fell down behind him. Surprised, the Hurons turned and ran toward the ridge where the others were hiding. Little Stone was impatient and tired from the long wait. He came down the ridge expecting to run into the Mohawks, but instead found himself entwined with the rest of the Huron. Sitting Owl paused when the two groups came together; things were rapidly getting out of control. The Huron crossed the creek and stopped when they reached a grove of aspens, birch and tag alders. Here, they took cover in the trees, and waited for an attack.

When the attack did not come, Little Stone said, "They have changed their minds. Lets start home; we've been away too long". Everything remained quiet as the Huron silently left the protective thicket of trees.

Sitting Owl delayed any further fighting that day. There was no advantage in fighting, and entering the thicket of trees would be too costly for lives lost. Instead, he drew back down the valley to take care of the wounded, and to make arrangements for their return to the village.

It was noon the next day when Sitting Owl reached the thicket where he saw that the Hurons had left. He was now a half day behind, so he quickened their pace. At his side, the river merrily babbled as it rushed by the stones and the obstacles that were in its way, until finally coming to rest in a deep, dark pool of water that was home for speckled trout at its head, and brown trout in the deeper parts where they lay protected by large stones..

The Indians continued upstream following the trail along the river. The trail pulsated on its course: at times next to the river, and then veering away until once again they rejoined sides. Rounding a sharp corner, Sitting Owl signaled everyone to stop. Ahead, there was a river falls that had broken free from a series of cliffs. Its stream cascaded on, until caught in deep pools encased in rocks. This falls was called Trenton Falls; it had a two and a half mile gorge, formed by a violent chasmal rift; the river flowed at its base and over many years, its channel deepened as it flowed through a limestone bed.

Red Feather spoke, "There is a trail that we can follow, and it goes to the top of these cliffs. We are familiar with this river, and have come many times to a falls we call Kuyahoora",meaning 'leaping water'* (*Sherman Falls is where runoff water in the spring causes the water to shoot out horizontally from the face of the falls.)

Sitting Owl replied, "The cliffs would be a good hiding place if the Huron plan to return to the Mohawk Valley. It would not take us long to climb the cliffs to see if they are there".

Upon reaching the top of the ridge, Sitting Owl looked down at the river. He could see quite a way upstream. The river entered the gorge and twisted and turned in its quest to leave. The water was dark, and the current swirled among rock formations with whirlpools in some of the pools. The drop of the river was evident by the number of falls in the gorge; each one spectacular and different, as it tumbled over limestone shale.

Far above an eagle, a speck in the sky, circled and Sitting Owl spoke, "Look! The eagle is watching the water spirits for Orenda. Everything is quite peaceful. Let us waste no more time here, for the Hurons have turned off the trail somewhere below".

The Golden Era of Trenton Falls

THE "ROCKY SISTERS"

A CHARMING VIEW OF THE FALLS FROM THE CLIFF WALK

THE CASCADE OF THE ALHAMBRA WHERE THE WATERS "LEAP AND FOAM AND PLAY"

When the Mohawk reached the bottom, Sitting Owl took Red Feather, and they walked back along the trail to the corner where they looked for a sign that might have been left by the Hurons taking a side trail.

"Here Sitting Owl", said Red Feather, and showed him footprints on a narrow trail that branched away from the river. "We missed this the first time because of the brush piled at the entrance. This time I noticed fresh cuts on some of the limbs."

Sitting Owl felt a sense of relief. He would be glad to leave these mountains. The mountains were smaller than he was used to, and they were filled with windfalls from fallen trees that made walking difficult, and limited travel off the paths. Here fighting would be in individual contests rather than in unit maneuvers.

Ahatsistari had coaxed a chipmunk to take acorns from his hand when Sitting Owl and his group emerged from the ridge's path. He watched Red Feather point out the Huron trail to Sitting Owl, and without delay, he left to return to Little Stone to warn him he was still being followed.

Sitting Owl found the tree where Ahatsistari had been sitting, and said. "This is a foe worthy of respect; he is the eyes for the others".

"Let us hurry", one said impatiently.

"Hough!" said Red Feather, "If it was up to you we would have charged into the Huron waiting for us back at the bend".

Sitting Owl again spoke, "It would be foolish of us to charge into a band of Indians when we do not even know their size, but this is not why I have held back, but rather it is that if we get too close, they will likely kill Bent Feather".

Little Stone was standing on a trail in an isolated part of New York State. This trail had been used in the past by Huron war parties, who crossed the St. Lawrence River, and traveled overland in New York State. Little Stone, after leaving the mountainous region, would continue overland, travling northwest upon a plateau, This path would keep him safely away from Iroquois towns, and take him to the shores of the St. Lawrence near its outlet from Lake Ontario. Iroquois fishing and hunting parties came to the rivers and streams flowing into Lake Ontario, to coincide with seasonal migration of fish and ducks. Little Stone hoped to avoid contact as he was weary from the walking.

Little Stone spoke, "Ahatsistari reports that the Mohawks are once again in pursuit".

Twisted Nose spoke, "Our captive slows us down. We should kill him."

"No", replied Ahatsistari, "He is mine, and I will determine if he should be killed. The leader of the Mohawks keeps a distance because he hopes we will not kill him".

That evening, when both groups stopped for the day, Sitting Owl kept jogging along the trail until he reached the Huron camp. Indians on the warpath arose at sunrise and stopped at sunset. He quietly went around a Huron sitting on the trail keeping watch. Sitting Owl noiselessly circled the edge of the Huron camp staying inside the tree-line. He saw who he felt was Bent Feather; his feet were shackled (probably bound with basswood fibers); there was no sign of other prisoners. He circled back to the path. The Huron on guard had fallen asleep while sitting and leaning back against a tree. Sitting Owl fingered his knife, then he crept silently away.

The next morning Sitting Owl addressed the group, "It is time we move forward to attack". Murmurs of agreement could be heard.

"Yes", said Chattering Squirrel, "Let's attack, and end this chase".

Diving Otter spoke, "The Hurons must learn they cannot attack one of our villages without retributions."

Sitting Owl said, "Let us go then, but be careful lest we startle a bees nest!"

Little Stone stood debating. The trail divided; one went due west, the other due north. He looked at Laughing Gull, next to him, and said, "I, with part of our warriors, and the prisoner, will take the north path. You leave with the warriors you select, and be decoys, so the Mohawks will be fooled into following you on the west path".

Laughing Gull selected several braves, then motioned for Ahatsistari, who was carrying their single musket. Laughing Gull stopped after a short distance upon the west trail, then signaled for everyone to seek cover in a stand of beech trees surrounding a small clearing.

Soon the Mohawks came into view. Ahatsistari fired his musket before they had come into bow and arrow range. Sliding Arrow fell with a howl of pain. Sitting Owl tried to get his men into a position to fight; but time and time again the rifle barked when a Mohawk rose up to rush them and claim a coup.

Finally, in frustration, Sitting Owl redrew with his men. Now he realized the need for this new weapon; he looked at the Indians gathering around him. They were all young. If he had had older, more mature braves, they might have been less impetuous and they may have claimed victory. With a saddened heart, Sitting Owl signaled his men to turn around and start back.

The Huron rejoined forces and continued due north (today, the Huron trail overland can be traveled following Rt 28, author). Bent Feather watched the Indians unite and knew that his friends must have been unsuccessful. Ahatsistari came over and was more relaxed. Bent Feather could understand the Hurons' speech because they were Iroquoian-speaking, like the Mohawks.

Bent Feathers decided it might be a good time to ask Ahatsistari about the similarity between the two nations speech. He also wished to know how much farther it was to their village.

Ahatsistari explained, "The Huron are the main stock, with the five Mohawk tribes originating from it". "Now we are headed for our village", he said. "We are one of two groups; the other group went by water with prisoners; we took the overland route. We are about two weeks from the St. Lawrence River, and then we are about three to four more weeks from our village."

"How did you get so good with the musket", asked Bent Feather?

"By the pale face traders whose faces are covered with hair," said Ahatsistari. "They showed me the muskets when I was younger, and they watched while I fired and reloaded. I even learned a few words that they spoke, 'si voux ple'". "Now that your friends are leaving, maybe you would like to tell me why you followed us alone?"

Bent Feather looked sheepish, and said "My sister was captured, and I was following to find her and help her escape".

Ahatsistari said, "Then she must be with the larger group coming by a water route. We went the old overland route to leave a trail that the Mohawks would follow. We did not plan on capturing prisoners until we stumbled across you sound asleep," and again Bent Feather looked sheepishly down.

During the next few days, the Huron started to come toward Bent Feather. One of them said, "Do not worry Mohawk! Soon we will build a fire and roast you for a fine meal."

Another laughed, "You will be the center of attraction in the village when we all gather around you in a circle, and have you dance and sing for us".

Still another taunted him holding a stick to his chest. "When I do this the next time, it will be lit and red hot".

The land grew level as they approached Lake Ontario and its tributary, the St. Lawrence River. By taking the north trail, they avoided the Oneida, and would come out on the St. Lawrence River.

Ahatsistari stood with Bent Feather and said, "See the creek; it is flowing north toward the St. Lawrence instead of south into the Mohawk River. Soon we will be across the great river, and will be in the forests with villages of the Onontahataronon who are Algonquin, and live with the Huron in the winter.

Bent Feather, cautious not to slip on the clay bank, looked out on the flat land, fields extending as far as he could see. Geese were in formation, flying overhead. There were all types of ducks; one appeared to be painted it was so pretty. This was a wood duck that would nest in the bogs and marsh each spring. Ahatsistari stood quiet and respectful as Bent Feather looked all around him in awe.

Then Ahatsistari spoke, "One of my closest friends died in an attack upon one of your villages. His mother has no one else at her fire and I have spared your life so that you might be her adopted son." Like the Mohawks, an adoption must be approved by the clan mother, who undoubtedly, will confer with the boy's mother before approval. "Soon we will cross the river and return to our village. We will need to get through carries and marshes on our trip. We pass by numerous Algonquin villages whose braves are our allies. You will be kept blindfolded in the canoe, so that you can not easily repeat your journey from here to Huronia".

Their journey was a three to four week strenuous and difficult trip. They would (leaving present day Trenton) embark on the Trent River; go down to Rice Lake; then up the River until they were forced to carry around Burleigh Falls, through Buckhorn into Bobceyaeon Sturgeon Lake; pass by Fenelon Falls into Balsam Lake; then finally follow a creek leading to Lake Simcoe which marked the Eastern edge of Huronia. (Today canals and locks have eliminated carries; there is a waterway for the entire trip.)

Bent Feather walked with Ahatsistari into the Algonquin village across the river. The village did not have the long houses of the Iroquois village,but instead it had dome shaped houses with birch or woven mats placed over a framework; then tied with strips of wood to hold them in place. The Indians would move in the winter to a forested area that had small game, and a lake that allowed ice fishing. Then in the summer, they would live where they could hunt big game.

Ahatsistari pointed out a scaffold that was holding an Indian body, and said, "Like us, they collect and clean the bones for a ceremonial burial in mats of bark every ten years. They believe that two souls are controlled by Manitou (a supernatural being,) and that divinity resides in all creatures and objects. (Hessler) We will stay long enough to eat, then Little Stone will have us continue our trip home."

When they entered Lake Simcoe, they looked toward the southern boundary of Huronia. The land continued until on the northern side you would see Georgian Bay. Bent Feather could see the land was only slightly hilly and there were many lakes and villages. There was just enough wind to make the lake ripple with intermittent white caps

Trent Severn Waterway

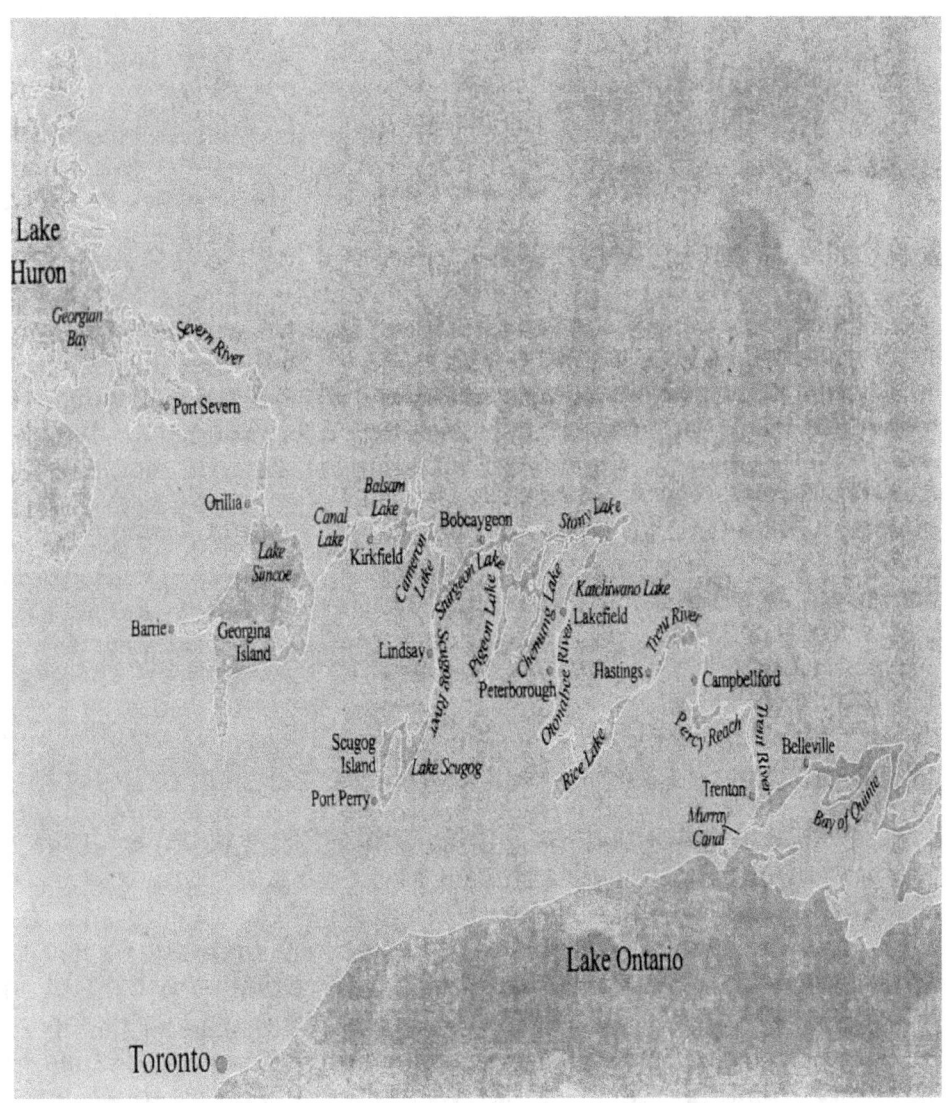

Chapter V - The Mohawk Attack (September 21, 16

Sitting Owl returned to the village after his unsuccessful attack. The villagers greeted the braves as they entered. One, a War Chief named Thunder Cloud, approached Sitting Owl. He spoke, "Welcome back! Although you were too few in number, it was good you tracked behind the Huron."

Sitting Owl replied, "We were repelled by musket fire,and I am sure it was caused by one of our muskets that was taken during the capture of Bent Feather. I am also sure that this Huron received instruction on how to use it from the french traders."

Thunder Cloud replied, "That is bad news, but it will not change our invasion. Our party is larger and will attack from all sides." "We are leaving with the approval of the clan mothers."

True to his word, he left the village the next day, departing by canoe. Sitting Owl accompanied them and described where he found the trail following beside the West Canada River; and how an attachment had been hiding in Fulmer's Creek to entrap a Mohawk war party.

Thunder Cloud said, "I have traveled different routes, and will cross Lake Ontario at the western end into the land of the Neutrals. Then we will go straight north. This will keep the Algonquin villages to the far right. The group you chased will also be to our right, so they will not expect us when we arrive.

Thunder Cloud did not know it, but this was similar to the route that the Huron had taken with the prisoners.

When Thunder Cloud reached Onondaga Lake, he chose Sitting Owl as his delegate to go to the Onondaga Village, and see the War Chief over the five nations. He carried a few black shells, which indicated the decision of the war chief of the Mohawk confederacy to declare war in retribution for the Huron attack.

The five confederations were a loose organization, and often acted independently. Thunder Cloud did not plan to wait; therefore, he left Sitting Owl, and continued on his way toward the Neutrals' nation, which was in the heart of the Huron country. He decided to continue northward, and attack the southern Huron outpost called Teanaostaiae.

Three weeks later, the Mohawk looked out from the edge of the forest at the fortified outpost. Huron villages were Iroquoian, and were designed the same as the Mohawk'. The palisades walls were double thick. Suddenly, with streaks of light breaking forth at first dawn, the Mohawk rushed the palisades with terrifying screams.

The Huron awoke but were overrun, and the fight was quickly over. Thunder Cloud lined up the Huron prisoners, then left for home. He would use these as prisoners to exchange for the Mohawk that the Huron had taken as prisoners.

They returned the same way that they had come. Thunder Cloud could see no reason not to. They passed close to the Neutrals' village, Aendironon, which bordered the Huron territory. It was heavily forested, and there was a good supply of fruit and nut trees, and berry bushes. It was fall and time to harvest the produce. The Neutral's were fierce warriors who declined to get involved in the Huron-Iroquois conflicts. Thunder Cloud was aware that there were eyes peering from the woods watching them as they skirted the Neutrals' lands, but no braves confronted him.

Chapter VI - Sitting Owl & the Dutch (October 1614)

Wilhem DeGroot looked over the table, that was made from split logs with poles used for the legs, at his friend Henri Bakker and said, "I believe that the Mohawk are trading some of their furs with the French."

Henri spoke, "We can only collect the furs for the New Netherland Company. They limit the terms that can be used to barter for the furs."

As Wilhelm re-lit his pipe, which had gone out, he said, "We need to travel among the Indian nations and villages and get to know them on a personal basis."

"Yes", replied Henry, "The Mahican have furs and first traded with Henry Hudson while he was onboard his ship on the river. One of their villages is just across the river from us now."

Wilhelm contemplated before responding, then took a deep draw on his pipe and said, "The Mahican and Mohawk both wish to trade, and they were blocking each other. They both need our tools and weapons. We cannot control events from here; we need to visit the villages and hold talks. I will take Peter Bacon with me and leave in a fortnight."

"Good", said Henri, "meanwhile, I hope they do not have a war between themselves; that would be dreadful."

The next morning Wilhelm and Peter left to visit the neighboring villages. They had awls, beads, cloth and cooking utensils for the women; and blankets and knives for the chiefs. A light snowfall had begun as they started up the Hudson River toward Schenectady.

Sitting Owl sat in the sweat lodge and sprinkled a decoction* prepared from Solomon's Seal's roots, which he had found at the edge of the forest last spring; it's branches gracefully bent in servitude toward it's violator. He inhaled the smoke, which rose in the steam from hot rocks placed into the water, and felt relief from his persistent headache. There had been no word about Running Doe, so Sitting Owl decided to spend a few days at his mothers. He brought two deer with him, and she made him new leggings and a new pair of moccasins which extended above his leggings. *(made by boiling roots in water)

While there, Sitting Owl decided to go west to the other nations to try to see if they might have heard any word about Running Doe.

The next morning he was up and on the trail when a familiar figure approached him, waving and wearing a big smile. It was Wilhelm DeGroot who, also, was going west after he left Schenectady. With the help of an interpreter, he told Sitting Owl his plans to visit the Mohawk; and he was going to talk to them about trading with the Dutch. Then he asked Sitting Owl if he would like to accompany him.

Sitting Owl replied, "I am going west for information about my wife, and will keep you company until you turn back. I must continue on my own journey."

Wilhelm explained he was going village to village to try and convince the Indians that the Dutch would give them the best price; and to have them promise to trade only with the Dutch. To convince Sitting Owl to join him for the talks, he gave him one of the blankets he had brought. Sitting Owl thanked him, That night he slept fitfully because he dreamed about a forest that had no wildlife, and seemed to hear an eerie moaning from pines as the animal spirits wailed in sorrow.

When he woke, he was more sure that it was wrong to overkill the Creator's creatures, and upset the wilderness spirits who had, for so long, kept things in balance for the Indian. Little did he know the future when Indians would be fighting for existence as they were caught up in supplying beaver furs, and the white man would be instrumental in instigating so many of their fights

Sitting Owl took Wilhelm to each village and while they were there, they talked with the villagers. He asked about Running Doe, but no one had heard anything. The Indians in all of the villages were glad to see the Dutch and accepted the gifts they were given. In return, they gave them much food, usually some furs, and would join them for a short distance as they left to go to the next village.

Chapter VII - Bent Feather in Huronia

Bent Feather was in a longhouse in the Cord Clan that was surrounded by villagers. Chief Stands Alone stood and said, "Singing Bird, you lost your son in our recent battle, this is Bent Feather, your adopted son; Bent Feather, this is your new mother, and you will now be known by the Huron as 'Sleeping Bear'."

The Clan Mothers conferred and agreed to the adoption. Singing Bird walked over to Bent Feather and took his hand. "Welcome, my son", she said. All the Huron gathered around and clapped and shook his hand. Bent Feather felt happy over all the fuss made over him.

That evening as they sat around the fire, Ahatsistari came by, and said, "Welcome to the Huron tribe, my brother." After he sat down, he continued, "This is the Cord Clan, one of the four original clans. About the same time as the Iroquois League united; two Huron Clans: the Rock Clan (Arendahronon) and the Deer Clan (Tahontaenrat) came from the St. Lawrence and joined the Bear Clan (Attiginawanton) and the Cord Clan (Attigneenognahac). Later on, a fifth grouping joined us, as did other nations, in fear from being attacked. This village is Ossossane." "For a while you will be kept close to the village but soon there is a group that is going to visit the Illini Indians to our west, and you may possibly join us."

"While we are there, we will talk about trading furs, and you will meet some of the French Trappers, who visit us during the winter months" "Oh, I meant to tell you. A very pretty Mohawk escaped from our main party and took refuge in a Neutrals' village. The Huron left her alone since she had a newborn, and she found a chance to slip away. The Huron went to the Neutrals', but they refused to let her go because she was Mohawk, and they said they would only let her go with the Mohawk."

Bent Feather was speechless. Had he come so far for nothing? His only hope seemed to be to somehow make his way to the St Lawrence and find a Mohawk war party on the river. Then he would have to make his captors think he had gone back to the south on the same trails that had brought him here.

He walked down to the shore of a nearby lake. He looked around the lake and noticed that it's trees grew down to the water. He focused on a fallen log out in the water, and near it something dark in the water. Something was swimming and he was studying it when a youth his own age joined him.

"Do you see that?" He asked.

"What is it?" asked Bent Feather, who was unsure.

"That is 'Old One', a moose who comes each fall because this is where the cows gather. We try to kill him each year but his spirit is very great. Whoever kills him will also be great indeed. By the way, my name is Sitting Bear"

Bent Feather replied, "I am called Sleeping Bear by the Huron."

The two boys crossed the lake in a canoe that the Huron kept hidden in storage until it was needed. It was birchbark, and the waves generated by breezes lapped gently against its side. The fall colors of the forest were at their peak; many were bright red sugar maples. Intermingled were the yellows and browns from the oaks, beech, and poplar.

Once across the lake, they found the tracks where the 'Old One' had left the water. Many tracks led to the base of a hill, whereas only his set of tracks led up the hill.

"Here" said Bent Feather, "The big moose comes down the hill in the evening, joins the others at this spot, and leaves them here in the morning to return up the hill by himself." Sitting Bear watched Bent Feather as he continued following the Old One's tracks; a faint impression on the ground which he stooped over to study; a tuff of hair impaled on a twig; a stone overturned: nothing escaped his attention. "Look", said Bent Feather and pointed at a large oak, the "Old One has rubbed his antlers against that tree. It appears he has used it more than once. We should climb upon a limb and be waiting at sunrise when he returns by himself."

"Let's sleep outside tonight", said Sitting Bear. They built a temporary shelter from balsam branches, and fell asleep listening to an owl hoot from a nearby tree.It was still dark when they awoke and climbed into the tree. It was not long before they were both dozing, stretched out on the large limbs of the tree. As dawn approached, they were awakened by the birds singing.

The sun broke over the horizon and its rays struck the Old One as he approached the tree, and it created a sheen that radiated off him. "Surely that is the Great Spirit", said Sitting Bear. Both boys climbed down, and hurried back to the village where they were met by Ahatsistari.

"Your mother is worried, Sleeping Bear. Go to her so she knows you are all right." Ahatsistai listened to their story about the Old One, and was surprised at what he heard. He said, "It would seem that the Great Spirit was protecting the Old One by shielding him. Very few have seen him."

Later that day, Bent Feather met two French trappers who had come to their village. "Bonjour", said the first one and then continued to talk to him in the Huron language, "You are Mohawk, are you not?"

"Yes", said Bent Feather, "I am."

"We are returning through Huronia to Quebec", said one of the Frenchman. "We see Mohawk war parties on the St Lawrence, but many of your braves are in the south fighting the Susquehannocks, who are a fierce enemy. Maybe you are better off with the Huron who are excellent traders and businessmen." With a wave, the two turned and left.

Deep in thought, Bent Feather sat by on the shores of Georgian Bay, and watched the sunset that night. He did not return until the purple sky deepened into darkness.

Chapter VIII - Return of Running Doe (November 1614)

Sitting Owl was having his morning cup of bedstraw when a Seneca currier stopped in front of him, and greeted him by name.

He said, "I am Seneca. They call me Rumbling Bear, and I bring you good news, Sitting Owl. Your wife was brought to our village by the Neutral Indians from their village Ongniaahra." (*This is the present day site of Youngstown, New York State.*) "She is with a group of Seneca who were picked to escort her to you. Come, I will lead you to them."

Sitting Owl jumped up, grabbed some hominy cakes, and could hardly constrain himself. Rumbling Bear took one of the cakes and said, "Let's get going. I will eat this on the way." They left on a narrow trail that was well defined, and easy to follow.

The sun was still in the East when they met Running Doe with her escort of braves. She ran to Sitting Owl and jumped in his arms. He held her tightly and said he would never leave her alone again.

That night after finishing a large meal prepared by the Mohawk for Running Doe and their Seneca guests, Running Doe turned to Sitting Owl and told him about her ordeal.

She had been taken by the Huron at the riverside while watching for Sitting Owl's return from Fort Nassau. She could hear screams of victims intermingled with cries of the Huron. Soon everything was quiet. Canoes were launched with prisoners. After they had departed, a second group left signs for the Mohawk to follow going overland. And that was the group Sitting Owl had followed.

The Huron continued their escape by water using caution: they stayed close to the shore and kept their scouts on land along the shore. Luck was in their favor and they passed through Oneida Lake without seeing any Iroquois. They crossed over Lake Ontario and landed in Ontario ahead of the group that held Bent Feather as prisoner. Running Doe was not bothered because she had her infant with her, and many times she was able to stand off to the side, unnoticed by anyone.

Once the Huron were across Lake Ontario, they headed towards Kandoucho, a neutral village to the North near Huron country. It was dinner time when they reached the village, and they stopped for the evening. Now that they were near their Huron homes, they were more relaxed and ate a large meal, and soon everyone, even the guards, fell asleep.

When they were asleep, Running Doe told how she escaped. "I walked away. I took the trail back for a little way, and then I hid off to the side. I carried some chamomile with me to make a tea to keep the baby quiet, and I gave him a little bit. They searched for me, but could not find me, and after they looked for me for a day, they gave up. I found some partridge berries to eat, and sucked on a cone of sumac berries, which gave me some fluid. I followed the trail back to the Neutrals' Village, where I was taken in. The villagers said they would make sure I was returned to the Mohawk. They told me they would send me to a village that was near the Senecas' village. And that, Sitting Owl, is pretty much my story."

Chapter IX - Sitting Owl made Sachem

Painted Bird was a Royanch (title-holding) woman and sat with the other women around a fire in the council room. She spoke, "Many of the young men wish to go on the war path against nations to our south. The Dutch keep after them for more and more furs. Sitting Owl has spoken about not killing too many, and has said 'Orenda watches down on all his creation. He has provided for us to live, and is happy when we thank him in our festivals. This has been our way, and I fear his wrath should we change the ways of the old, and he becomes unhappy with us.'"

The council debated and decided that they would recommend that Sitting Owl become a Pine Tree Chief;(i.e, advisor to the Council of the Five Nations). He would become elected by this Confederate Council, since he had a great interest in the Nation's affairs, and was a trusted and honest man.

Chapter X - Attack on the Munsee – Delaware (1615)

It was a sunny day and Sitting Owl sat on top of the notch. He had a panoramic view of the village from this vantage point. The river was be-ginning to skim over with ice, and soon it would be frozen making canoe travel impossible. Sitting Owl often rose at dawn and would leave for the notch. He stretched and felt a presence. Turning, he watched Thunder Cloud come toward him, then sit down beside him. Sitting Owl said to him, "The war parties have returned from the St. Lawrence?"

"Yes", said Thunder Cloud, "Until next spring when we can return again with small parties who will harass Huron along the river bank, and disrupt their supply of furs to Quebec."

"My grandfather used to say the otter who tried to keep two fish in his mouth was most likely going to lose one", said Sitting Owl. "I fear too many war parties are out."

'Ah'. said Thunder Cloud, "so he ate one at a time." "Each war party knows what it must do."

Sitting Owl sighed,"You may be right, I hope you are."

Thunder Cloud remarked, "We have already left the Hudson for the adjacent headwaters of the Delaware and the Susquehanna Rivers where beaver are numerous in the small streams. The Munsee, just to the south of our lands, live along and claim the Delaware River as their own." "The Susquehanna, although Iroquoian who speak like us, do not wish to let us trap along their upper streams."

Sitting Owl commented, "The Munsee have their own dialect although they call the Delaware their grandfather, and they may have an Algonkinian connection."

They were silent for awhile until Sitting Owl spoke, "To our east where we are the door keepers, the Micmac are fighting the Penosbscot. Although the French moved across the Bay of Fundi to build Port Royal on Micmac land, they still traded with the Penobscot. This caused the two to declare war. It seems that my dream is coming true and the dark clouds are just beginning."

"Many braves have gathered the furs that they will need in order to trade for muskets; we will leave for Fort Nassau to obtain them, then we will go to the small streams of the Susqueanna and Delaware Rivers", said Thunder Cloud. "We shall establish our right to use the tributaries and small streams that flow into the rivers. By the way, Sitting Owl, do you have anything I can use for a cough?"

Sitting Owl replied, "Come, we will get some inner maple bark and make a tea to take for your cough. I will also give you some dried bloodroot, which is also used for a cough, which I do not wish you to do just before attacking the enemy."

Thunder Cloud asked, "Are you sure you do not wish to come?"

"No", said Sitting Owl, "I will return, once again, to the St. Lawrence and watch for Huron parties that dare to use the rivers for passage to Quebec City."

"Good", said Thunder Cloud, "I will make sure the Munsee (Delaware) and the Susuehannocks do not try to deny us using their rivers' headwaters for hunting and trapping."

The next day Thunder Cloud left with 30 braves. They would go overland to the Schoharie Creek and then follow it upstream until it turned south easterly. Then it would be a short walk to the west to come to a stream that flowed into the Delaware River. There were two inches of snow on the ground; they walked silently, single file. Overhead the oaks and beeches rose majestically; their clinging snow falling at random to the ground as limbs and branches warmed in the sunlight .

Thunder Cloud had many young braves, including Sitting Owl's youngest brother-Running Fox. He drew the braves around him after they reached the headwaters of the Delaware, and spoke, "We are heading towards the Munsee council village Minisink. We will come close to the village but we must stay hidden in the woods. We will try to catch the small groups who leave the

54

village headed out to hunt. Then we will take them captive, and return to our village."

"These headwaters flow into the Delaware River which turns to the east. There will be Mahicians and Wappingers to our north and east, and Susquehannocks to our west. We must be careful not to let our enemy get between us and our home. If this happens, we will split up into small groups and sneak between their lines."

"Ha!", said Slippery Eel, "If that happens, we will let Running Fox run and have them chase him. Then we can slip through in the confusion."

Running Fox retorted, "If they catch you, they cannot hold on, because you are too slippery."

Thunder Cloud held his hand up, "You are a fine pair, now let us get back to the situation at hand."

The Mohawk followed the Delaware River as it wound easterly towards New Jersey. When they reached a big bend in the river they knew they were not far from Minisink . As they approached the village, they moved silently through the woods. They stopped at the edge of the woods to look at the village. The Indians lived in dome shape wigwams made with saplings and bark. Remnants of corn tassels remained – evidence of the women's work in the fields. Since they were Algonquin, the Mohawk language was not interchangeable. The Indian braves carried heavy war clubs fastened around their waists letting the Mohawk know this would not be an easily defeated nation. Thunder Cloud let his braves examine the village from the forest edge, and then led them back into the recesses of the forest.

The village came to life at daybreak. A small group of braves met so they could go hunting, and they were waiting for one more brave to join them. His name was Pale Deer and he was frequently late. The group of Indians waited for him a few moments, then they left the village. They were unaware of the Mohawk who had seen them leave, and were now following them until they find an opportunity to attack.

Pale Deer, called Slothe for being routinely late, was irritable. He had hurried, but had still been left behid. He knew where the others were going and decided to take a shortcut through the woods and meet the others at a large field. He came upon the Mohawk bedsite, and although not knowing what tribe had stayed there, knew he must warn his friends. Thunder Cloud, following the Munsee group, sent two men to scout ahead and find a good place to attack. They returned to tell him that a good place would be just before the path opened into a field. Thunder Cloud directed Mohawks to lie in ambush on both sides. The Munsee group was surrounded and surrendered. Pale Deer watched from the far side of the field. There was nothing he could do, except return to his village for help. Back at Minisink, braves gathered around while he spoke about his friends' dilemma.

An older brave at Minisink spoke, "With these grey hairs comes the wisdom of many years. Have a group leave early when it is still dark, and have them hide in the woods off the trail. When a second group leaves in the morning, the Mohawk will follow them. The group in hiding, shall wait for the Mohawk to pass by, then strike from the rear." The Munsee chief, Eagle Feather, approved this plan, and quickly appointed two groups.

Thunder Cloud could hardly conceal his glee the next morning when he saw another group leave, like the one had left the day before. He followed, a safe distance back, so that his group would not be detected. Something was making him feel uncomfortable, and he mentioned this to Croaking Frog who was an older brave.

Croaking Frog said, "They are moving too fast for a hunting party. It is as if they know we are following them."

Thunder Cloud said, "I will send out scouts to keep to the side of the Munsee group, then we'll see what they might discover."

Thunder Cloud called Running Fox, and said "Pick a few Indians, and make sure there are no other Munsee lying in ambush."

When Running Fox was up front, getting ready to turn back, he noticed movement in a bush in front of him. He quickly dove for cover, saying to his comrads as he fell, "This is a trap. Go back to the main group."

Eagle Feather was in front with his group when the Mohawk split sending scouts to the side. Caught by surprise, he raised his head so he could see better. This was the movement Running Fox saw. Realizing they had been seen, Eagle Feather rose and signaled his men to charge into the Mohawk.

Thunder Cloud was instantly aware that another group of Munsee were positioned ahead of him. They had been tricked into following the group leaving the village. His Mohawks shot a volley of arrows into the Munsee, giving time for his scouts to rejoin him. Then he led the Mohawk further back into the woods as the two Munsee bands joined forces. The Munsee, with war clubs raised and with howls of anticipation, rose to charge. The Mohawk used bows and arrows to slow the charge, then continued retreat into the woods. Cries of derision could be heard getting closer when Thunder Cloud saw a hill. The Mohawk fled to the top and turned around to shoot at the Munsee. Shooting at the Munsee downhill soon had the Munsee at a disadvantage. The Munsee returned to the bottom of the hill to regroup so they could try again to charge the top.

As dark approached, Thunder Cloud gathered his braves together and said, "We must go to the Delaware River; the moon is full and we may have enough light to walk to it." The Mohawk cautiously left when they saw the Munsee fires lit at the bottom of the hill. It was steep on the side of the hill that was unprotected, so they began a slow and cautious descent. The moon was high in the sky, when they saw the black ribbon of the Delaware looming in front of them.

Thunder Cloud led his group down the Delaware until they came to a point where another river flowed into it. This river was called the Lackawaxen River. This river flowed westerly and toward the Lackawanna River which flows into the Susquehanna River.

Not far up the Lackawaxen River Thunder Cloud stopped and lined his men up into a defense line. "The Munsee will follow", he said, "and we will wait here for them until tomorrow."

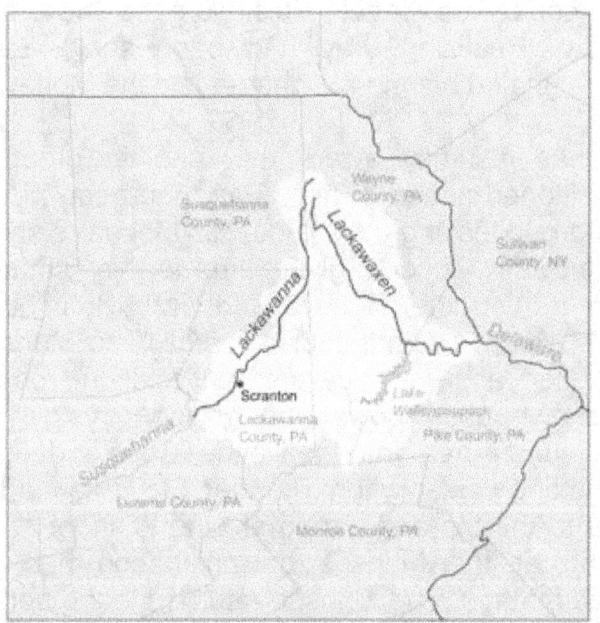

They did not wait long before the Munsee appeared. This time the Mohawk rose, and with bloody whoops ran into the Munsee brandishing tomahawks and warclubs. Thunder Cloud, in the lead, twisted and swung like a demon. The Munsee broke and ran in terror. Thunder Cloud did not delay, but quickly started for the Lackawanna and the Susquehannock River with half of his original force. The Indians were somber as they returned.

Thunder Cloud stopped on the headwaters of the Susquehannock, to trap furs. He said to his men, "We will get muskets for the furs, then we shall return again to Minisink."

Chapter XI - Huronia visit to the Illini (April 15, 1615)

Bent Feather sat on his favorite rock overlooking the Georgian Bay. "How very different this is from our Mohawk Valley." he mused.

Sitting Bear came and sat beside him, and could hardly restrain his excitement as he said, "Sleeping Bear, have you heard, many men are going to the Illinois Indians' land, and some of the older boys are going too."

"Hmm", said Bent Feather, "I hope I may go also; let's find Ahatsistari and see what he knows."

The two youths found Ahatsistari checking his birchbark canoe for possible leaks. The Huron canoes were birch bark, and lighter than the Iroquois elm bark canoes, which were heavier and more cumbersome to use. The Huron relied on their canoes to navigate the streams and lakes of Huronia. The Iroquois tended to walk more.

Ahatsisteri stopped working on his canoe, and said "We will not leave until May, when the streams are free of ice. Standing

Stone will be in charge of our group and I will put in a good word for both of you. It will be good for you to travel to the west and take part in the talks that will allow us to trap more beaver for the French in Quebec. Now since we will be leaving for a while; we must hunt so that we can leave enough meat to last until we get back."

The time passed quickly with much to do before they departed. Then the villagers came to watch the Indians leave. They carried their canoes to the edge of the water, and set out in them. These canoes were large; eight to ten Indians could comfortably fit in them.

The Georgian Bay

The Indians launched their canoes at Georgia Bay and skirted the islands as they traveled west. Four days later, they passed through the Straits of Mackimac, and entered Lake Michigan. They would follow the west shore of the lake until they came to the tip of Illinois at the bottom of the lake. The first tribe they would visit were the Kaskaskias, who were located in the north-eastern part of Illinois. Bent Feather knew that they were Algonquian, like most of the tribes in Canada.

They were almost to the village before the villagers were aware of their arrival. Then the villagers poured out in greeting. Bent Feathers struggled to pick up their dialect. Ahatsistari, who was alwsys alert, said, "They speak a dialect similar to the Miami Indians. But, beware of the man who looks down and does not look you in the eye. These people are timid but treacherous.

However, we will smoke the peace pipe so we can get an agreement to trade with them for beaver."

"Most tribes to their north are their enemies and make war upon them, such as the Shawnee, Fox, Dakota (Sioux), and Kickapoo." added Standing Stone,

The Kaskaskia led the way to their village. The village consisted of oblong huts covered with mats of rushes and was so tight that neither rain nor snow could penetrate. Each hut had four to five fires that accommodated eight to ten families. Fields were being prepared to plant corn and squash. Once the fields were planted the groups would break apart and go to hunting camps.

The Cahokie and the Tamaroas tribes both lived in central Illinois along the Mississippi. The Huron left Kaskaskia to go to these villages. The Peorias, who lived in the northwestern part, would travel to Cahokie. The Kaskaskias traveled with the Huron for aways from their village. Standing Stone, who did not trust them, kept a guard posted during the nights they traveled together.

Buffalo

Bent Feather caught Sitting Bears attention, and pointed to large humped animals with shaggy fur. "What are these?"

Ahatsistari said "They call them bison, or buffalo. The Illini hunt them. If we are lucky and the buffalo herd has not left by tomorrow, maybe we can join the Illini in a hunt."

Next morning the sun broke free and rose as a red ball over the horizon. Both boys grabbed their bow and arrows, and waited for the Illini to appear. Soon a party of Illini came, and one approached the boys carrying two extra wolf skins, used as camouflage. "Here", he said "Carry these and follow me." The Illini left at a fast walk and the boys were almost running to keep up. About a half mile from where they had slept, they came to a flat, grassy field. The two boys gasped at the site. Buffalo were grazing on the field as far as the eye could see. The herd followed an old buffalo who led them steadily towards the rising sun. The Illini guided the boys towards a younger calf that he had spotted away from the herd. He motioned for the boys to follow him, and, keeping close to the ground, they crept closer.

At the illini's signal, the two boys put on the wolf skins, and stood up. The young buffalo eyed the boys, but did not show any fear. The three advanced with arrows in their bows and all shot together. The buffalo staggered, then ran a few tottering steps until collapsing upon the ground.

Meanwhile the Huron and Illini formed a long line beside the main herd. At the chief's command, a barrage of arrows were shot. Many buffalo collapsed on the ground; the others began to run; they picked up speed until they were in a wild stampede; making the ground shake and tremble.

Afterward, the women went onto the field and began to cut up the buffalo. All of the parts of the buffalo would be used. After being skinned, the hump of the buffalo would provide meat for the feast this evening. Strips of the muscle, called jerky, would be dried in the sun, and a mixture of fat with the protein, called *pemmican,* would be their nourishment when eaten on the trail.

Bent Feather and Sitting Bear watched as the women stretched the hides while they were out on the prairie. They began by scraping off the fat, and they would smoke the hides to make them waterproof. With the fur left on the skin, they would provide winter robes, bedding, clothing and had many other uses.

Still, other hides would be prepared by removing all fur along with the fat. Then they stretched the skins over a frame, so that it could be reshaped by wetting and drying. This is called

rawhide which serves as food, clothing, drum covers, belts, and knife cases.

That night tee pees were assembled, and the Illini prepared a temporary camp. The fire burned brightly as the Huron and Illini passed the peace pipe. This testified to the good will between these two nations.

Afterward, a feast was prepared, and Bent Feather and Sitting Bear ate until they could not move.

The next day the Huron packed up for their return trip. The paths of the Illini would be open for use by Huron in their fur trade.

Chapter XII - Champlain's Seventh voyage (March 1615)

Samuel Champlain looked at the honeycomb appearance of the ice on the river. The ice would soon break free, and he was getting an urge to explore the wild and untamed forest. He had already drawn maps of the Ottawa River in 1613. Now he wished to chart the rivers to the west going toward Huronia. With the Iroquois making travel difficult on the St Lawrence, an inner network of streams would be beneficial to keep the furs coming in sufficient quantities. Impatient to get ready, Champlain turned to check on the three canoes, and Indian guides he sought for the trip.

April approached and Champlain had only been able to get two canoes and one guide. He made preparations to leave by May when he had "sufficient companions" to begin his journey.

May 1ˢᵗ 1615   Champlain's Journal

Day 1- We left Quebec City and went down the St. Lawrence to the Ottawa River and stopped where the river's drainage forms Lac Saint-Louis. I am accompanied by Etienne Brule and a party of Huron.

Day 2 – Shortly after leaving Lak Saint-Louis, we enter the beautiful Lake of Two Mountains followed by two bays. Their water sparkles with sunshine (St. Placide Bay and Rigaud Bay). Shores are heavily forested and fowl is plentiful.

Day 3-7 – Rivers flowing into the Ottawa are numerous and the overall water added is significant. We are already encountering Algonquins along the river.

Days 8-12 – Canoes and supplies had to be carried when we entered the frequent rapids and cataracts, with travel made more difficult due to the dense forest. We have not seen any Iroquois since entering the Ottawa River.

Day 13 – We stopped at an Algonquin village and were greeted with friendship and presented with a feast.

Day 14 – Close to the village another river enters the Ottawa River. This is called the Mattawa River, and our Huron say it is from Objiwa-meaning "a meeting of the waters." Indeed some of the most strenuous portages are where we follow the stream up to Trout Lake, a narrow seven mile long body of water. We have turned from the northerly direction of the Ottawa and are now going west.

Day 16 – We come to a larger lake, called Lake Nipissing, and we will follow a river (French River*) which flows out of the lake*(a 68 mile stream.) Heavily forested, rocks and ledges sharply define the shores of the river.

Day 30 - We have come to the shore of a large lake (Lake Huron), and this part of our journey ends at Georgian Bay.

Georgian Bay Samuel Champlain greets Huron Indians

June 1st 1615 Journal entry

Day 31- We are standing at Simcoe Lake, Southern boundary for Huronia. The Huron wait for a group of men to return from the Illini land. At this point I would like to talk about the Huron when traveling. When on the trail they eat only at sunrise and sunset. They usually add water and berries to corn meal for their meal. Sleep is to lie on the bare ground with the black flies insufferable in June. If you do not understand the Indian language, the hours seem prolonged. Caution: do not pick up a paddle unless intending to always paddle. The Huron always keep their first opinion of you that they form on the trip.

Day 37 – A Huron party of 80 or so men have returned to Huronia. One of the braves, although young, has a reputation for being one of their better warriors. His name is Ahatsistari. The Huron plan to attack the Oneidas and seek our help.

June 15th 1615

Day 44 – I expect 300 Huron will go on an attack. In addition I have about ten Frenchman. The Huron, during the past week, have been painting themselves and working themselves into a frenzy by doing the war dance.

Day 45 – We left Huronia and went straight down toward Lake Ontario. We will travel by canoe through the Kawarta region of waterways and the Trent regions to the East end of Lake Ontario. (*Same path taken with Bent Feather as a captive.*)

Day 60 – Huron chiefs advise going down Lake Ontario to the Oswego River, then going upstream to the Oneida River, and stay upstream until arriving at a stockade fort at Nichols Pond containing Oneida Indians.

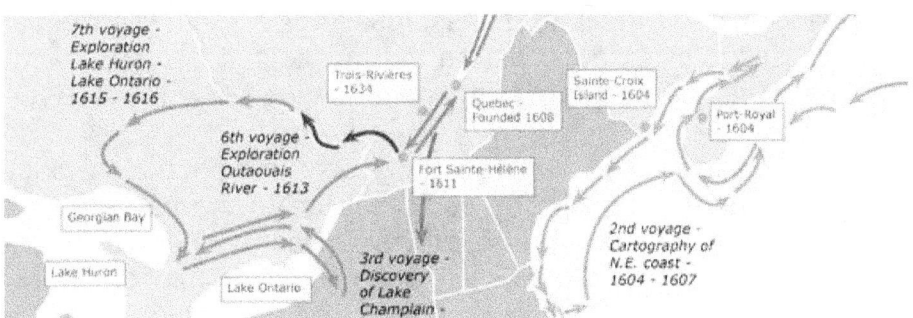

Samuel Champlains voyages North America

Chapter XIII - The Attack

Nobody questioned why Bent Feather had joined the military expedition. He was considered Huron by now. The closer Bent Feather got to the rolling hills in central New York, the more he considered his chances for escaping back to the Iroquois. For now he remained close to Sitting Bear so no one would suspect his plans. It was when they got close to the Fort that he saw his opportunity. All the Huron gathered around the French who were designing their battle plans. Bent Feather ducked into the brush and circled around to the back of the fort. "I am Mohawk, let me in", he said to a sentry. The Oneida Chief was called, and he listened as Bent Feather told of the plans to attack the fort.

When the Huron entered the clearing they saw several of the Oneida lined up outside the Fort. Contrary to the French wishes to remain out of sight until the next day, several skirmishes were held. The French fired their harquebuses, and the noise and balls whistling by sent the Oneidas into the fort.

Samuel Champlain disclosed his plans: to build elevated wooden platforms, higher than the palisades of the fort, upon which the French could stand and fire their arqueouses*. The next day the platforms were rolled into the clearing outside the Fort. The Oneida were able to shoot many arrows from the palisades, four deep and crisscrossed at the top with ramparts accessible by ladders, before the muskets' fire forced them to dismount and only fight from under shelter. *French muskets*

The French urged he Huron to carry large wooden shields protecting them until they could set fire to the palisades. Instead they fought in the traditional Indian manner, rushing the walls, and shooting arrows without doing significant damage.

The Huron did attempt to set fires which were inadequate and ineffective. The noise from the Indians made talk with the French impossible, so the French, upon seeing such a state of disorder and unruliness, withdrew from the field.

The battle was over, three hours after beginning. Samuel Champlain was wounded twice in the leg, one in his knee. (Champlain, 1632)

July 4th

Day 80 – Journal Entry : Battle lost. Huron prove to be undisciplined and do not take orders well in battle. Once I washed my wounds the Huron had me place plantain over the wounds before dressing them. It seemed to help. If difficult for me to travel, I will stay with them over the winter. (Champlain did stay with the Huron for the winter)

Chapter XIV - The Encounter

Bent Feather took a deep breath of air and felt exhilarated. By night he should be back in his own village. He had alerted the Oneida in time, so that they were not surprised by the attack on their village. It was a beautiful day with the sun filtering through the pines leaving lingering probes of sunlight.

Someone behind him spoke and he froze; slowly turning, Ahatsisteri, holding a notched bow and arrow, was not over twenty paces away. "Ah, Sleeping Bear, or is it Bent Feather today; tell me, from which side of the forked tongue does the serpent speak."

Bent Feather found his voice, "You are brave to be so close to the Mohawk land, Ahatsistari."

Ahatsistari said, "When I woke you up that morning long ago, you forfeited your life to become my prisoner. Now you have rejected the new life I gave to you. Now because you forfeited your life long ago to me, today you must die."

Bent Feather made a feeble effort to withdraw an arrow from his quiver, but did not have time to notch it in his bow; instead, he saw Ahatsistari draw the arrow back in the bow to release it and felt it pierce his chest. Falling, he heard Ahatsistari say, "Do not worry, you will be found here." He felt a searing pain in the crown of his head, then sank, falling into a bottomless black pit.

Later that day, a Mohawk paused by the body, and looked furtively around. Already, Ahatsistari was gaining a reputation of a grim, silent apparition that struck silently, then quickly to disappear into the cover of the forest.

Chapter XV - Years of Turmoil and Contention (1615-1625)

1615

Sitting Owl was going over his supply of medicines when Thunder Cloud entered. "Ah", said Sitting Owl, "How are you?"

Thunder Cloud looked at his friend and replied, "Your face tells me something is wrong."

"I have just received word that there is something taking place with the Micmacs; who upon defeating the Penobscot (Abenaki tribe) after an eight year war; left to invade the eastern coast."

Thunder Cloud replied, "Yes, that started after the French moved their trading post from the mouth of the St. Croix River across to the Bay of Fundy. It is called Port Royal." There was silence for a moment, then Thunder Cloud added, "Although now in Micmac land the French continue to trade with the Abenakies and the Penobscot."

"Well", said Sitting Owl. "It was brought to my attention that when the Micmacs swept down the East Coast, they encountered a new type of illness that almost destroyed them." "Now the Abenakies must be a major supplier of furs."

"Actually, no" said Thunder Cloud, "The St Lawrence is now the main route for the fur trade and it is the Huron and Algonquin that have benefited."

Thunder Cloud said, "When we took Munsee-Delaware captives after the first battle, we heard word that a new settlement had been started in Jamestown. Words spoken between the English settlers and the Powhatan Indians have spread up into the Chesapeake Bay region."

"That is far from us", said Sitting Owl. "We have the security of the nearby mountains, but we are surrounded by tribes who would like to see us succumb to them in battle."

"Yes", said Thunder Cloud, "The Dutch provide us with plenty of guns so that we can fight and gather furs for them." We are also a buffer zone between them and the French who trade with the Huron and Algonquins." "The Mahicans hold land on both sides of the Hudson and require tithes from us so we can take our furs to Fort Orange (Albany)."

Sitting Owl scowled and said, "After the fall hunting is over, we will discuss the tribes around us; and as the leaves fall from the trees; so shall our warriors spread out in the forest and seek victory."

"As the leaves swirl in the wind, we shall fight many tribes", said Thunder Cloud. "By the way, what is that plant you are holding?"

"That is Echinacea. It will will help keep you strong and healthy when on the war path", said Sitting Owl. "I hope that the sickness the Micmacs endured will not be repeated, where scores of people die. I have had no visions from Orenda, the Great Spirit. Tomorrow, I shall return to the forest and continue my search for a cure."

New England tribes (see map)

The original Algonquian-speaking inhabitants of Connecticut included:

the Mahican tribes (including the Pocomtuc)
the Minisink (Munsee) tribe
the Mohegan tribes (including the Niantic)
the Pequot tribe
the Nipmuc tribe
the Ouiripi tribes (Mattasbesic, Paugusett and Schaght)

riginal inhabitants of Pennsylvania include

the Erie tribe
the Iroquois tribe
the Lenape tribe
the Munsee tribe
the Shawnee tribe
the Susquehannock tribe

The original inhabitants of Massachusetts included:

the Wampanoag tribes (includingthe Massachusetts, Nantucket,Pennacook,Pokanoket and Pocasset)
the Mohegan tribe (including Nipmuc)
the Mohican tribe O9zincluding the Pocumtuc)

Chapter XVI - The Susquehannocks (1615)

The Susquehannocks were an Iroquoian tribe who had most likely migrated from the north, since they were friends of the Huron. Forced southward by the Mohawk during earlier years, they began trading with the Delaware. Etienne Brule, emissary for Samuel Champlain, visited in 1615, and found that the Susquehannocks were willing to trade with both the French and the Huron.

This became known to both the Dutch and the Iroquois, and soon the two were meeting in council. Wilhelm DeGroot, longtime friend of the Mohawk, joined Sitting Owl, and others, in a longhouse where council was conducted. They began by giving thanks to Orenda, the Great Spirit. Sitting Owl threw some tobacco on the fire with the smoke, and said "Each spring we sprinkle tobacco in honor of the 'Thunder Children'. Now I sprinkle tobacco to pacify the spirits with whom we depend on each day, and especially the Sun God, our Eldest Brother, who looks down on us with favor during times of war." <vii>

After the Peace Pipe was loaded with tobacco, it was lit, then passed around. The four directions, North East, South and West were acknowledged followed by Mother Earth and Father Sky.

The Dutch were praised as the Mohawk friend, and then Wilhem rose and spoke. "Our brothers, the Mohawk, bring us many furs for which we are thankful. So too, do the Mahician. Although Susquehannocks come with furs, we hear that the French and Huron are trying to get the Susquehannock to trade with the French. If they reach an agreement, you will be surrounded by French who travel freely among their Huron friends, and they will try to limit your trade with us."

Thunder Cloud spoke, "The Susquehannock must keep watch over the Delaware who are also on the lower part of the Hudson, and are between them and the Dutch at Manhattan. We will pass to the side of the Munsee (Delaware) Indians and not cross into their territory."

Sitting Owl joined the discussion, "The Delaware are poorly organized and weak. We have fought the Susquehannock over the last few years for hunting rights on the headwaters of their river. They are strong and fight well. How will our Dutch brothers help us, should we take up the war path?"

Wilhelm stood and held a musket. "This is a wheelock and more improved over the matchlocks you currently have.It is more reliable and instead of relying on a slow burning wick, it has a wheel grinding against a material that sparks to ignite the powder in the musket." He went on to demonstrate how to fire the musket with the Indians crowding around. He demonstrated how to replace the flint if needed to supply a new spark.

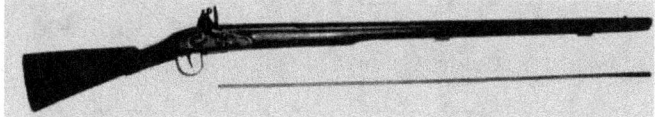

Chapter XVII - The Invasion

Wilhem stayed overnight with the Mohawk. Sitting Owl saw no alternative other than to continue their close friendship with the Dutch. The women met in council, and conferred agreement with the men. That evening as they gathered around a large fire, the braves began a war dance. Painted with red and black, they moved quickly through the dance routine with exaggerated movements; with the crescendo building as the dance progressed.

The next morning Sitting Owl was pleased to see Wilhelm join the expedition. "You are indeed our brother", he said. Wilhelm smiled and said: "The braves who have muskets may need someone to help them learn how to fire them."

Thunder Cloud led his force quickly down the Hudson to the headwaters of the Susquehanna. There he set up camp for the night.

He planned to follow the river and continue until he came to one of the villages they built along the river. The villages were fortified, but his force was large enough to directly assault their walls. Although muskets were plentiful, many of the braves only had bow and arrows.

Sitting Owl joined Thunder Cloud beside the Susquehanna River and spoke, "They will also have guns." Both sat quietly listening to the river's water rushing merrily by, unaware of the barriers further downstream, as the river continued its journey toward a sea full of unabated energy.

"We will strike their outposts first", said Thunder Cloud. "And we will sweep all of those who are in front of us. They were joined by Running Fox, who left Wilhelm sitting by the fire, smoking his pipe.

Sitting Owl looked at his younger brother and said, "Soon we will be in battle; some will seek a coupe by rushing forth; deeds may be sung by the fires, but remember, it is the pack of wolves that will bring down it's quarry." As the sun sank in the sky, it quickly became dark, and the Indians fell asleep. A coon paused by the riverside to observe the forms on the ground, then continued down the stream when all remained quiet.

The Indians rose in the morning at sunrise, and ate hominy cakes. This would be their diet for the rest of the trip. Soon they began walking on the trail beside the riverside. The first village encountered was a temporary camp used for hunting and fishing. It was empty, and Thunder Cloud signaled for the braves to continue along.

Late afternoon found them at the first main village, Thunder Cloud beckoned for Sitting Owl to come over to him and said, "Take some men and stay hidden at the back gate for a dawn attack".

Sitting Owl left as directed, and soon he and his men had faded from Thunder Cloud's sight into the expanding forest shadows. Midway around the village, Sitting Owl halted and pointed at a narrow trail used to enter or leave the village. "Look," said Sitting Owl, "The jackals have an escape here". Then taking a few men, he followed the path to the bottom of a gully where it ended by the side of a brook." It is a path to get water should they be held under siege", said Sitting Owl with respect.

Sitting Owl picked several Indians to lie on top both sides of the gully. All remained quiet until a rustling sound was heard coming up the path. Soon, several Indians became visible. Sleeping Owl was content to let this hunting group pass. He waited, but the Susquehannocks stopped and were peering at the rim above them. Sitting Owl did not not know what had alerted them to possible danger, but dared wait no longer. He gave the order to attack.

Outnumbered, the Susquehannock, who towered over the Mohawk in height and size, fought bravely. The Mohawk released a flurry of arrows into the ravine, then they jumped down to their foe, swinging their hatchets and war clubs. Thunder Cloud entered the fight, and the Mohawk quickly gained the upper hand, forcing the Susquehannock to surrender.

Thunder Cloud discussed the fight with Wilhelm and Sitting Owl. Running Fox had been wounded, and would miss further action, but would be left in the rear to guard prisoners.

"They know we are here now", said Thunder Cloud ."We will begin at dawn, and let the braves with muskets shoot at anyone seen on top of the palisades. We will form an assault team, and open up peep holes so we can fire the muskets into the village. Stories over fires will retell our bravery this day".

At dawn, a group of Mohawk sprang from the woods and ran toward the walls. At the same time, a barrage of musket fire spat off the walls and catapults. The Susquehannock leaned over the wall and men with white uniforms were seen. "They have the French with them," whispered the Mohawk. With extreme fury, they attacked the walls. As one fell, another would take his place. They quickly chopped through the walls with the iron axes they had received from the Dutch.

The Mohawk poured into the village, and many fell when a volley of musket fire greeted their entry. Soon it became hard for the Susquehannock to continue fighting because the Mohawk had the advantage of more men. A few of the Susquehannock had escaped through the back. Thunder Cloud gathered all the prisoners, including six Frenchmen, and started back. The Susquehannock would come back to pursue them, and Thunder Cloud had already lost a third of his men.

The Indians did not stop until they were near the Hudson River in New York. That evening several large fires were built and the French were led out. One, a rather portly man, was selected and tied to a stake. Soon screams began and lasted throughout much of the night before they waned; then they finally stopped, bringing an end to the torture he had endured throughout the night.

Next morning they continued on to their village. Wilhelm said good-by to Sitting Owl, and added "We accomplished our mission. The French will not pursue trading with the Susquehannock this year after our attack." Sitting Owl nodded in agreement, and looked from the village toward his cherished Adirondacks where he found solitude in its peace and quiet.

The next five years brought relative peace without any major campaigns. The Susquehannock moved a little further south, and the Mohawk and Mohican maintained an uneasy peace.

The New Netherland Company failed and was replaced by The Dutch West Indies Company (DWIC). Originally it was formed to seek Spanish shipping through piracy, then it was further expanded to include trade. It's ships would stop along the West Indies coast to seek slaves for the plantations.

The coastal tribes, such as the Wappenger and the Metoac, developed hostility over ensuing conscriptions by the sailors. They experienced a high mortality rate because they could not adapt to captivity and impoundment to which they were subjected.

Chapter XVIII – The Iroquois Council (Fall 1616)

Sitting Owl sat on the banks of the Mohawk River. A year had passed since they had invaded the Susquehannock with Dutch approval and assistance. The Mohawk and Mahican continued to live together in a fragile peace. The Dutch West Indies Company was now in place, Wilhelm DeGroot had returned to Holland. The DWIC encouraged land purchase and development unlike the New Netherland Co. who primarily had been interested only in trading.

Sitting Owl saw a storm begin to materialize on the ridge across the river. Flashes of lightning lit the sky for a few minutes, then all cleared. "The Thunder boys must have been happy with what they saw", said Sitting Owl. "The storm ended quickly."

Soon the tribes would gather around the council fire, already lit in preparation for the meeting. The Mohawk would sit on one side with the Seneca, and have three decision making parties. One party would monitor the other two remaining parties for correctness in procedure. Decisions were referred to the Seneca, who would then go over the wording, then the case would be referred to the Oneida and Cayuga. Finally, the Onondaga was given executive power to approve or reject the decision. In either case, it would finally be returned to the Mohawk, who could override all and leave it as the original decision. The Mohawk, who were the leaders, would announce the decision to all of the people at the council.

Sitting Owl felt his body relax and his mind become open to all people. Removed were the restraints, anger and deceit, shackled to him . He was free from prejudice, and ready to vote for the welfare of his people. He took out a string of sacred wampum and looked at the ridge where the Thunder Spirits had cleansed the air, and he confessed all of his wrong doings.

As time for council drew near, Sitting Owl knew he would emphasize the need to maintain the traditional rituals which he had learned so well as a child. (Gayanashagowa.)(n.d.).   viii

Chapter XIX - An Uneasy Quiet - (1616 – 1624)

The Mohawk and Mahican kept an uneasy truce. The Mohawk paid tribute to cross Mahican territory, and the Dutch traded freely with both tribes. During this time the Mohawk harassed the Huron on their annual trading trips to Trois Rivieres and Quebec, and would lie in ambush along vantage points on the Ottawa and St. Lawrence Rivers. Sitting Owl listened intently to stories brought back about Ahatsistari, and his feats as a warrior. He listened without comment when Running Fox told how with only fifty braves, Ahatsistari had made three-hundred

Mohawk flee. Sitting Owl knew he would take one more trip into Huronia, and he would seek out Ahatsistari to avenge Bent Feathers' death.

It was during this time that Fort Nassau was abandoned because it was prone to flooding. A new stockade was built close by on higher land.

Mohawk war parties left once more, treading upon the Mohawk Trail that would lead them down the Hudson. In later years they would follow this trail into Massachusetts and Connecticut. Mahican war parties also started north on this same Mohawk Trail, and the two tribes clashed in physical contests under the canopy of oaks and beech, some would remain lying upon the forest floor that was cushioned by years of falling leaves.

The Dutch were able to use their past support of the Mohawk by supplying muskets to them in their struggle against the Susquehannock, and they negotiated a peace between the Mohawk and Mahican in 1618. The Mohawk listened to the Dutch when they met by the council fires. The women also conferred, and spoke about diminished numbers of men in the longhouses. This time there would be an end to the fighting.

1620 saw the settlement of an English colony in Plymouth. Soon there would be another country seeking its own fur monopoly, and adding to an already shifting pattern of alliances and supply of muskets, which enabled the Indians to continue fighting. Both the Mohawk and Mahican were finding the beaver in decline, but the Mahican had an additional valuable resource: wampum that was found on the lower Hudson. The Dutch, learning of its importance, began seeking wampum in lieu of furs.

The Dutch West Indies Corp. saw an influx of immigrants arrive and purchase land from the Mahican who owned both sides of the river. Sympathies began to be expressed for the Mahican, and they were asked by the Dutch to arrange trade between them (the Dutch) and the Algonkin and Montagnai. In 1624, fires burned brightly in the Mohawk village council longhouses, and young braves danced war dances around the fires while the elders voiced their discontent.

Chapter XX - The Mahican (1624)

The Mahician was an Algonquin tribe that lived in the Hudson River Valley, that stretched from the Catskills to Lake Champlain. Two tribes, the Wappinger and the Metoac, settled at Long Island and the Lower Hudson Valley. The Mahican, like the Mohawk, were frequently fighting, and like the Mohawk, were anxious to trade furs with the Dutch. The Mahecan owned the land around Fort Nassau and on both sides of the river.

Note: These were *not* the tribes written about in "The Last of the Mohecans'" by John Fenimore Cooper. Rather they are a distinct group, who at one time included the Lepaut tribe, who had left the Hudson Valley and migrated to Connecticut.)

Crooked Arrow was a Mahican Chief in the Wolf clan, and chosen by heritage through matrilineal decent. He met at regular intervals with other clan leaders from the Deer and Turtle clans. Crooked Arrow beckoned to Mad Squirrel, an Indian who came over to join him. They were in their capital, Shodac, located just opposite of Albany. Mad Squirrel, whom Crooked Arrow had never seen mad, was the tribal War Chief.

Mad Squirrel said, "The wind that blows the leaves to fall has carried visions of Mohawk hiding in the swirls." Crooked Arrow looked at him thinking that he said this every year when he would leave with scouting parties, and go deep into Mohawk territory.

"Maybe he is a little mad", thought Crooked Arrow who said, "Go to the Dutch and get muskets for each of your men. This should be possible since the Dutch wish us mediators for their upcoming trade agreements."

"Yes", said Mad Squirrel, "and I shall also ask for the new flintlock rifles." Bidding his friend good-by, he said, "First I must go to our Medicine Man, Black Cloud, who is waiting to chase any evil spirits away from me that may be close by."

*War would occur upon the decision of the Sachem (chief) and his Counselors. Then the Heroes, that have proven to have courage and prudence in war, would take over the execution of the war, and continue until peace is proposed.

Chapter XXI - War and Alliances (1624 – 1635)

New Amsterdam - NY City (7AM)

The Dutch gathered to discuss Indian affairs. They were in a new trading post called Fort Orange, that had been built on the other side of the river. This made it easier for the Mohawk to have access when they came. Timothy VanButte had been in some of the Mohawk villages, and he spoke, "Fires are lit in the Mohawk lodges, and there is unhappiness."

"Why?", asked one of the Dutchmen.

"Furs are getting scarce where both the Mohawk and Mahican trap. We asked the Mahican to arrange trade with the Algonkin and Montagnais in the St. Lawrence Valley." Timothy said as he stoked the fire and watched the embers rise, "The Mohawk have been enemies of these two tribes for a long time. They do not wish to trade with them."

Several of the men began to whisper among themselves, and Timothy could see sentiment building for the Mahican. One of these was the Fort Commander, Krieckbeck.

Peter O'Tool said, "Let us travel south down the river to New Amsterdam, and trade with the Indians down there while these two engage in battle. The Dutch West Indies Corp, was overheard saying that a new fort in New Hampshire is possible, and it is right near a Pennacook Village." Peter stayed for a few minutes with Timothy; who were both alike in temperament and attitude, and they got along well together.

Chapter XXII - Otstungo – Mohawk (7am)

Sitting Owl was taking advantage of his free time to sit with Running Doe. Both were sipping bedstraw, their morning beverage, over which they discussed their plans for the day.

"There will be men to stay in the village", said Sitting Owl.

"I only worry about you", said Running Doe. "It has been a long time since you have left for the war trail."

"I will be back when the Thunder Spirits call, heralding the season of rebirth." Sitting Owl missed the former levity and humor that Running Doe had, before she was taken by the Huron.

"Come", he said to his eleven year old son, "You must keep a sufficient supply of arrows handy, and do not leave the village by yourself." Then he got out his war paints. He would need more yellow paint than he used in the past, since he was now an elected sachem.

Chapter XXIII - Schodack - Mahican (7am)

Crooked Arrow was hoping that Mad Squirrel would return soon. He looked at a bag containing belts and strings from different tribes, that were used for tokens of peace. It was Crooked Arrow's job to establish peace with them. Helping him to do this were elected aides, and, if faced with war, they would give a hatchet to the War Chief who took over the responsibility for the war. At the end of the war, Crooked Arrow and his assistants would take charge, and negotiate peace.

Rolling Stone, one of the counselors', sat with Crooked Arrow and said, "Do we still have the tribes who are pledging their friendship?"

"Yes" said Crooked Arrow, "We have the Pennacook, Algonquian allies, living by our side, the Pocumtucs who live as our neighbors and have an Algonquian dialect like us, and we also have the Sokoki as friends. The Sokoki live with the Pocumtucs in western Massachusetts along the Connecticut River."

"The Abenakie and the Sokoki, who are sometimes called Western Abenakie, have long been enemies of the Mohawk."

Rolling Stone said, "It would seem that we have the Mohawk pretty well surrounded, for the Abenaki and their confederates are to our North, and the Mohawk can expect no help from the Abenakie."

Crooked Arrow watched as the smoke swirled into the sky and said "Ahh, the Mohawk come with the falling leaves, without warning and sudden,and like the fallen leaves spiraling in a swift wind, they are ferocious to see." (Mahican history)

Just then a Mahican appeared from the forest. It was Mad Squirrel, and he was shaking his head when he reached them. "It is not good," he said. "I have gotten close enough to see many of the villages gather around their fires and dance the War Dance."

"So, as I suspected," replied Crooked Arrow. "I will tell the people that the hatchet will be turned over to you."

"Good", said Mad Squirrel, 'I will distribute the new muskets so that each group will have a few, and I will give them to the best marksmen." And with that Mad Squirrel left to begin taking charge of the war.

Chapter XXIV - Mohawk and Mahican War

Sitting Owl was in the front of the war party scouting with a few other braves. They moved stealthy in and out of the trees half way up a ridge that was above the trail, A movement and glimpse of something white, near the bottom, caught his eye. He dropped to his knees and his companions also kneeled.. Motioning for them to stay where they were, Sitting Owl crawled in a crouch down the ridge for a closer look. He suddenly froze. The white he had seen was a uniform. There was a war party of Mohican with several white men walking on the trail. Crawling back to the others he left two Indians to watch them from above while he and the rest returned to Thunder Cloud and the main force.

Thunder Cloud deliberated, "We must hurry because they will be here soon. I will take half the warriors and hide along side the trail, while you do the same on the other side. When they come down the trail, we will attack from both sides.

Sitting Owl lined up his men on one side of the trail, while Thunder Cloud did the same on the other. The Mahicans' first warning of an attack was when Thunder Cloud signaled for his men to shoot arrows.

Caught in the two lines of fire from both sides, the Mahican soon surrendered. That evening the fire burned brightly reflecting off the faces of prisoners. The white uniform spotted by Sitting Owl belonged to the Dutch Fort Commander, Krieckbeck, who was killed during the fight.

Chapter XVII - Fort Amsterdam (1626)

Peter O'Tool was walking outside the fort when he stopped to visit with one of the new settlers who had begun farming. He said, "Good morning, Daniel. How are things going?"

"Not bad", replied Daniel, but I am a little worried about the Indians who do not seem too friendly."

"Ah", said Peter, "I am afraid they feel we have taken advantage of them on land deals, and on occasion, we probably have. The Wappingers' were seven tribes loosely joined until conditions with the Dutch caused a tighter bondage."

"All three tribes, the Wappingers, the Unami and Metoac all share a related Algonquian language, so they can all talk with one another and all three share a common culture and life style."

Daniel said, "My neighbor told me that the Unami and Metoac are Delawares'."

"That is true", said Peter, "and they will not fight each other like the Mohawk and Mahician, but instead they will take up arms against us. That is why we cannot sell muskets to the Indians here."

Daniel asked, "How is that fight between the Mohawk and Mahican?"

"No sign of letup", said Peter, "Furs come from the Susquehannock, who are on the Connecticut River, then come through Massachusetts and Connecticut."

"By the Mohawk trail?" asked Daniel.

Peter slapped his young friend on the shoulders, and said "You are learning quickly. Soon we may come and get you and use you as a soldier rather than being a farmer," and with a smile he waved good-by.

As Peter was leaving, whistling a merry tune, Daniel spoke to Peter's back and retorted, "Not likely."

Chapter XXVI - Mohawk Trail

Thunder Cloud was satisfied with how things were going. One by one, the Mahican villages were falling. The Mohawk was using a direct assault method of attack. The Indians had designed a shield made of logs when running to the walls. This gave them protection from the guns, and once at the walls they would hack holes in the bottom. This would give them access to shoot into the forts, and provide them with an opening to enter the fort.

This would become riskier when towers were built outside the four corners of the fort, for it would allow the defenders to shoot down at the assailants by the walls with a cross fire,

The Mohawk had a well defined trail across central New York and it crossed the Massachusetts/New York line and then continued into Northern Massachusetts. (Note: The Mohawk trail is followed today by the New York Thruway and Rt. 2 in Massachusetts.) It opened the way for the Indians to attack quickly and gave them access to the Connecticut Valley.

Chapter XXVII - The Mohawk-Mohecan Fight is Over (1628)

The fight had lasted for four years. It was finally over. The Mohican had lost most of their territory on the western side of the Hudson river. No longer would the Mohawk pay tribute to cross the land. Now, instead, they would get stipends of wampum available from the lower Hudson, which was as valuable as furs and was used as barter with the Dutch. The land was still without many beavers, so the Mohawk continued to tread and hunt the Mohawk Trail into western New England, and remained on the warpath with the Mahican allies: the Pennacook, the Pocumtuc and the Sokoki. At the same time, the Mohawk looked to the North and the St. Lawrence where their old enemies, the Algonkin and the Montagnais, were located.

Sitting Owl looked towards the north knowing he would one day leave, and find Ahatsistari on the Ottawa River.

Chapter XXVIII - The Beaver Wars Begin (1629-1670)

Quebec City (1629)

It was morning, in the year 1629, and word passed quickly among the Quebec inhabitants. They gathered at the cities edge overlooking the cliffs. Below in the harbor was a flotilla of ships bearing English flags. These ships arrived before the French fleet, and they would block the French ships from landing. The English Commander, Sir David Kirke entered the city and took it over in the 'name of England'.

Noticeably absent among the spectators was Samuel Champlain. He had already left with others. The city would remain under English control for three years until the Treaty of St. Germain-en-Laye. During this time, French dominance would lessen along the St. Lawrence.

The Mohawk met in conference with all eyes turned North. Algonquin and Montagnais villages along the St. Lawrence had depended on French aid and trade. Now that the French support had stopped, the Mohawk, heavily armed by the Dutch, realized that this was now the time for them to attack.

Thunder Cloud said, "Let us send war parties large enough to take back what we have lost."

The rest of the Indians listened and voiced consent.

Chapter XXIX - The beginning of the Beaver Wars (1629)

Once again Sitting Owl left to go up north. Up the Hudson, then North on Lake Champlain to the Richileu River, which brought them to the St. Lawrence-- trade route for the Huron and Algonquin. Jesuit priests offered sanctity to the Indians who wished the safety of Quebec, away from danger of marauding bands of Iroquois, and they used muskets to entice their conversion. The Mohawk decided that the Algonquin-Montagnais trading village at Sillery, near Quebec, should be their target.

Sillery was awakened to a blood curdling cry. Bronze warriors, faces streaked with paint, ran into the village. Shots of muskets were heard over the screams of the victims. The villagers' were assembling a weak offense when a second wave of attackers struck from the rear. The battle, some say the first battle of the Beaver Wars, was over with all of the villagers' either killed or taken captive.

Thunder Cloud was exuberant. The Mohawk had very few casualties.

Sitting Owl was glum, and failed to feel excited over the battle. "I want to meet one warrior, a Huron who has slain many in battle. When I confront Ahatsistari, then I will feel content."

Thunder Cloud said, "I could send you up the Ottawa River with a scouting party, and you could watch for any Huron that may approach from that direction. The rest of us will stay in the St Lawrence Valley and reclaim the land we lost to the Algonquin and Montagnais in 1610." We will visit Trois Riviers* where I hear black-coated men offer their braves guns to follow them." *(Three Rivers)

"It is good news for us that they are divided" said Sitting Owl." We Mohawk are united with a strong tribal infra- structure. All have a part in our decisions around the council fires, and we leave with one mind."

Thunder Cloud turned to leave, "Be careful, Sitting Owl, for Ahatsistari is their greatest warrior and has killed many in conflict."

"Hoy", grunted Sitting Owl, leaving so he could be by himself and sharpen his ax.

Thunder Cloud selected a scouting party. He put Sitting Owl in charge, and they left to enter the Ottawa River to reconnoiter** the numerous villages along it's banks.**(gather information about)

91

Chapter XXX - Along the Ottawa River   (1632)

The Mohawk controlled the waterways, both the Ottawa and the St. Lawrence, and on this day had a war party numbering about three-hundred. They were looking for an Algonquin force reported in the area. Hissing Snake ran and said, "A small party of fifty Huron are close." Sitting Owl rushed back with Hissing Snake to see for himself. The party was landing and seemed to be arguing with the leader. There was no question as to who the leader was; tall with broad shoulders. It was Ahatsistari, who had grown, in the minds of many, to mystical proportions.

Ahatsisteri was firm with his group; they wished to run and fight another day when the odds were more equal. Not Ahatsistari! Had he not recently with fifty men in canoes beaten an Iroquois force of three-hundred?

He persisted and ended any further discussion. He led the Huron toward the larger force of Mohawk. Ahatsistari drove his men straight forward, intent on causing the Iroquois to lose formation. In the center of the melee, he came face to face with an equally tall Indian. "I know you," he said.

"Yes" said Sitting Owl, "The chase into Trenton Falls."

The two grasped each other and Sitting Owl knew he would be lucky to be the victor. Then an inner strength came, and a voice, like Grey Wolf said, "You must fight as the wolverine, thrust, twist, tear." Sitting Owl dropped to one knee and brought Ahatsistari's arm over his shoulder, and rolling, threw Ahatsistari over him to land on the ground on his back. Ahatsistari tried to rise, but Sitting Owl held him to the ground, and several braves rushed in to help Sitting Owl hold him.

Ahatsistari was a prisoner of the Mohawk. He stood, proud and unafraid of his upcoming ordeal. Sitting Owl saluted him for the great warrior that he was. Now Sitting Owl's war was finally finished, and he had avenged Bent Feather.

Sitting Owl would return to his village, and as the Sachem, he would look after the welfare of his people. He would sit on councils, address problems and he would try to reduce the number of epidemics that were beginning to pop-up in different Indian tribes. He would try to clarify what was causing events to transpire so violently and abruptly. And he would try to understand what the Indians were seeking that required so much war, and why the wars were necessary? With more and more muskets, the Mohawk was the dominant tribe, but the question was, whose benefit was really served; the Whites or Indians?

Chapter XXXI - Smallpox   (1633-1634)

Sitting Owl was concerned. A great number of Indians were complaining of headache and nausea, and when he looked at them, knew they were too warm with a fever. He recalled hearing about a sickness in 1617 being carried on an European slave ship, and how once infected, 90% of the Massachusetts Bay Indians died from it (Smallpox). Earlier between 1592 – 1596, hundreds of Senecas died from an infectious disease (measles).

Sitting Owl told his son, Red Fox, "I will need some plants from the forest. Listen to me, for there are several. I will need willow bark for fevers, wood sorrel leaves in case some have nausea, and look for Jewel plants."

 For topical use, I boil the plant down and save the juices. Let it cool. It can be applied to skin for relief of ecaema or poison ivy (Iroquois)

"What if some have headaches?" asked Red Fox.

"Willow bark is the best for that," replied Sitting Owl. "Bring witch hazel leaves and I will make a tea that can be gargled in the throat".

Sitting Owl was rapidly inundated by the number of those who were ill. Red Fox could barely keep up with supplies. Sitting Owl recommended that the sick ones use a sweating bath. White cedar, when steamed and inhaled, should bring relief for headaches and fever.

That night Sitting Owl slept by himself outdoors, so he could be closer to the sick ones. Running Doe had spent all day making the sick ones as comfortable as possible. Exhausted, that night she fell asleep upon one of the cots that was now empty, and had been formerly used by one who died from the sickness.

A week later Sitting Owl saw how red she was, and made her stop working. Flushed from the fever, he had her start using willow bark, and looking in her mouth saw sores. Leaving Red Fox in the village, he left to find more wood sorrel and get some leaves for the mouth sores. It gave some relief, but Sitting Owl could only watch as Running Doe, like all the rest, broke out with a pink rash over her whole body that turned into a raised and crusted rash. Helplessly, he watched Running Doe die from the smallpox epidemic.

Forlorn, Sitting Owl left to be by himself, sought word from Orenda. Once again, he slept on a bed of hemlock, and the stars overhead were his ceiling. That night he dreamed he was frolicking with the wild animals and running from field to field.

The next day, at the village, Sitting Owl found the chief, Morning Sun. He told the chief of his dream and vision, and how he had been alone nights and stayed healthy. "We must move from here to another village site, and escape the evil spirits that wish us to remain in this spot."

Morning Sun said, '"I will consider this", and turned and left. He envisioned the people leaving for a new site, but each time the field around him turned a red that flickered. That evening he stirred the logs to keep the fire burning, and noticed the red sparks rising up. He jumped up as he understood the meaning of the redness, and spoke to the villagers.

"Sitting Owl and I have sought advice from Orenda, the Great Spirit, and as in times past, he has shown us what to do. We must burn the belongings of our village, and move to a new site."

Smallpox kept ravaging the Indians, as did other diseases, including measles, scarlet fever and influenza. The Huron lost half of their fighting braves to disease between 1637 and 1641, and were overrun by the Mohawk in 1647 and 48. (Cengage learnings)

Chapter XXXII - Tumultuous Years (1632 – 1675)

1632 - 1650

Sitting Owl was back in his village. So too, was Thunder Cloud, who had been wounded, and taken back to the village for treatment. Thunder Cloud was not happy about being away from the battles, but realized he would not be effective as a war chief while he was hurt. Sitting Owl was having him stretch his leg and had provided a stick shaped so that he could lean on it while standing. He applyed a boiled, thin astringent of Speckled Alder Bark to the bruised area, and gave him Ginseng for energy.

The French were back in power in Quebec, and for the next decade they saw increasing hostilities and battles between the four main participants, the Mohawk, Algonquin, Huron and Montagnais.(Note: Details and battles can be found for this time period in the Jesuit Relations). The Huronia was destroyed at St. Ignace and then St. Louis, The Huron sought refuge with Jesuits on St. Joseph Island. This, too, was temporary, for they were ravaged by famine and a continuing war from the unforgiving Iroquois who killed many Huron seeking food on the mainland.

The Mohawk and Algonquin fought many battles. The Mohawk, now, had open access to the St Lawrence Valley, and they traveled where they wished. Although suffering many defeats, the Algonquin still remained a fighting entity.

French Jesuits were caught up in the war and were ultimately tortured and killed by the Mohawk. Smallpox struck the Huron in 1636-1637. By 1650 the Mohawk were practically raiding with impunity, throughout the St. Lawrence Valley.

Meanwhile, in New England, European powers continued their explorations. England began establishing colonies along the coast and by 1638 had built a trading post in NH in Pennacook territory.

The Swedes set up a colony on the lower Delaware River (1638) and the Susquehannock began trading with them. Four years later the Susquehannock were at war with the English colonies in Maryland. In 1643 the Dutch were at war with the Wappenger-Delaware, and together with the English, destroyed several of the Delaware villages in southern New York. The Munsee and Unami (Delaware) and Nimoac joined the Wappenger, and the Dutch sought assistance from the Mohawk and Mahican with whom they had previously established peace.

Chapter XXXIII - The Beaver Wars End   (1650 – 1675)

In 1650 the Mohawk began a campaign against the Susquehannock. It lasted five years and left the Susquehannock shattered. The Mohawk turned East and found a coalition comprised of Pennacook, Sokoki, Pocumtuc and Mohican that were joined against them. The Mohawk attacked the Abenaki in Maine because they helped the Montagnais. The Mahican, drawn back in war, were driven from the Hudson Valley. This left the fighting on the Pocumtuc who struggled for a year. After a failed peace attempt they were driven from the Connecticut Valley. In 1655 the Dutch defeated the Swedes, and in 1664 the English defeated the Dutch.

England made a treaty with the Mohawk who take up the tomahawk against the Pennacook and Sokoki (1665). They once more walk the Mohawk Trail through Connecticut and Massachusetts, on a path trod deep from the passage of so many moccasins. Although Mohawk offense is slowed by the increase in French soldiers in 1665-1666, the French seek peace with the Mohawk in 1667. During 1668, free from French interference, the Mohawk drove the Pennacook from their home in N.H.to Southern Maine, and the Sokoki were forced to retreat to the St. Lawrence River and the French protection. (Note: Olsen Allen and Rasmussen) The Pennacook became pretty much absobed by the Abenaki.

Blood shed continued in 1675 in the King Phillips War, but the Wampanoag delegation sent by King Phillip seeking Mohawk aid did not receive it. The Mohawk were quiet this time. The older warriors who had been in the earlier battles gathered in the council longhouses, and told the things they had experienced to the younger braves.

They told the young about the fear instilled in other tribes, when the Mohawk war hoop was heard. They told of tribes uprooted from their homes, and forced to flee from nations united against them. They told of nations pledging support only to break the bondage when it benefitted them. They told of the whites who coveted the land they saw and thirsted for its possession, and how they stripped the land of many of its resources.

Sitting Owl was very old, and used a cane, although the handle was very much like a war club. The young listened to his speech.

"It was many years ago when the first white men came seeking trade, and we helped them. At first it was good, but we soon learned that the Europeans wanted our lands and stripped it bare. We welcomed them to our council fires and listened to them reaffirm that we were brothers, but it was the Indian who fought. No longer can I look to the north and see the Huron, Munsee and the Delaware are silent to our South, and the Mahican have left. Now, that the Indians are weakened, we see whites increase in number and form their own militia driving out tribes from their homeland. The Pequot, who once filled Connecticut, were driven out by the English colonists." *(they had the help of the Mohegan and Narragansett*)

"We have fought many battles since that first battle long ago on the shores of Lake Champlain, and we have sought the whiteman's weapons. We like the way that they belch flashes of light followed by the sound of thunder pealing forth like the thunder gods. Orenda used to look down with favor when the Indians of old fought in the way he desired – competing in a conquest of strength. He has let the Thunder Gods darken the sky so he need not see us fight using their weapons. He is anguished over the loss of so many of his Indian children. and he is discouraged over the Indian's loss of dependence upon him which we had during earlier times, when he took care of our wants, and supplyed our needs in the forest so we might live. Now the whites crave our land, and deplete the forest of it's supplies. A pestilence follows them where they go, and we die in great numbers."

"I am very old and I leave you now, to go into the Adirondacks with only my bow, kinife and ax, and wait for the Great Spirit's call to come."

The others at the council watched him leave, shoulders straight, eyes fixed on the Adirondacks in the distance. Although not seen by those in back, there was a smile of contentment on his face.

author's note -- for a timeline of the Iroquois Wars (1533 – 1650) refer to bibliography (Evolution publishing)

Endnotes

iiiiii Dew Eagles are Supernatural creatures that fly above the clouds, and if they come to earth, it is only to alight on a mountain top. The only way they are seen is by dreams. They can be appealed to, though, through sacred tobacco.

iv Around 1700, trade goods were sold at the following standard prices by the Hudson's Bay Company. Ten made beavers*, properly stretched and cured, would purchase one gun. In addition one made beaver would purchase the following quantities of goods; one-half pound powder; four pounds shot; one hatchet; eight jackknives; one pound tobacco; one-half pound beads; or one good coat.

*A Standard of Trade was established, based on the made beaver (one prime beaver skin in good condition). Prices of all goods were set in Made Beaver.

v   He was a man who excelled and exalted in feats of war, yet in dying expressed hopes for peace. He was a hero to the 17th century Huron, yet in later years his name was given to a shadowy figure said to be the killer of those found mysteriously dead and scalp less in the woods; a bogeyman to scare young children into behaving properly. This man was Eustace Ahatsistari (possibly meaning 'He Cooks With Fire'),1 a Huron of the Cord tribe who was thought to be the greatest Huron warrior of his day.

vi   Fulmer begins as a trickle in the hills south of Little Falls, flows south towards Paines Hollow, turns northwest to Edicks (2.3 miles) and Days Rock (4.4 miles) before making a 4-mile descent to the Village of Mohawk (8 miles) and the Mohawk River (9 miles). For much of its length it runs side by side with Route 168 until it crosses Route 28 at the south end of the village. From there it flows through backyards and under side-street bridges before passing under the Main Street Bridge and easing into the river.

Vii When tobacco is placed into fire and becomes smoke: words become power, thoughts have physical substance. It is considered evil to misuse this power with severe repercussions for those who employ it for purposes other than prayer, thanksgiving or clarity of mind. Tobacco is so closely allied with humans it is called oionkwa:onwe-that is the same root word as human beings. It's Latin name is niotiana rustica and is very harsh and pungent, hence those who elect to smoke it may blend the leaf with gentler tobaccos or herbs.

Viii Indigenous Policy Journal Atonement among the Haudenosaunee (Six Nations Iroquois)

Bibliography

Gayanashagowa. (n.d.). *The Constitution of the Iroquois Nations.* Retrieved Ma 26, 2010, from Iroquois Constitution: html:file://K:\Iroquois Constitution.mht

Mshican   history.   (n.d.).   Retrieved   Aug   12,   2010,   from www.dickshovel.com/Mahican.html

Olson, A. &. (?). *Mahoican History.* Retrieved Jul 27, 2010, from History of Indian Tribes: http://www.dickshovel.com/mahican.html

unknown. (n.d.). *Eustace Ahatsistari he bravest of the brave.* Retrieved Aug 15, 2010, from www.wyandot.org/ahatsistari.htm

Laubin, R. a. (1977). *Indian Dances of North Americas.* University of Oklahoma Press: Norman and London.

Gayanashagowa. (n.d.). *The Constitution of the Iroquois Nations.* Retrieved Ma 26, 2010, from Iroquois Constitution: html:file://K:\Iroquois Constitution.mht

Cengage kearnings. (n.d.). Retrieved 05 2010, 09, from Encyclpedia of North American Indians -- Mohawk: http://www.college.cengage.com/history/readerscomp/naind/html/na_0231 00_mohawk.htm - 21k - Cached

Evolution publishing. (n.d.). *Timeline of the Iroquois Wars (1533 - 1650).* Retrieved 04 2010, 09, from http://www.evolpub.com/ACNA/ACNAChronology.html - 30k - Cached

Hessler, M. (1995 Spring). *Wicaz Review* , 41.

Catholic Nuns and Obijwa Sachems Louise Erdrich 'Tracks'.

Obijwa concept of soul dualism – each person possessed two souls which can metamorphize into other animate objects as they travel. 1> The Stationary soul resides in the heart and provides cognitive powers, emotions, and the ability to act. It can leave the body for a short time, but a long separation causes sickness-even death. 2>The Traveling soul dwells in the brain and exits separately from the body. It travels outside the person during sleep, and acts as the eyes for the stationary soul.

www.ingramcontent.com/pod-product-compliance
Lightning Source LLC
Chambersburg PA
CBHW081402280526
45788CB00009B/2959